# The Professional Serial Killer and the Career of Ted Bundy

# The Professional Serial Killer and the Career of Ted Bundy

✦

**An investigation into the macabre ID-ENTITY of the Serial Killer**

*Bonnie M. Rippo, Psy.D.*

*Illustrations by Anthony Aguilar*

iUniverse, Inc.
New York  Lincoln  Shanghai

# The Professional Serial Killer and the Career of Ted Bundy
## An investigation into the macabre ID-ENTITY of the Serial Killer

iUniverse books may be ordered through booksellers or by contacting:

iUniverse
2021 Pine Lake Road, Suite 100
Lincoln, NE 68512
www.iuniverse.com
1-800-Authors (1-800-288-4677)

ISBN-13: 978-0-595-42384-2 (pbk)
ISBN-13: 978-0-595-86720-2 (ebk)
ISBN-10: 0-595-42384-1 (pbk)
ISBN-10: 0-595-86720-0 (ebk)

Printed in the United States of America

To the Children of Today and Tomorrow

# *Contents*

Preface . . . . . . . . . . . . . . . . . . . . . . . . . . . . . . . . ix

**CHAPTER 1**     Introduction . . . . . . . . . . . . . . . . . . . . . . 1

Background of the Problem . . . . . . . . . . . . . . . . . . . . . . 1

Statement of the Problem . . . . . . . . . . . . . . . . . . . 3

Purpose of the Study . . . . . . . . . . . . . . . . . . . . . . 3

Theoretical Framework . . . . . . . . . . . . . . . . . . . . . 4

**CHAPTER 2**     Literature Review . . . . . . . . . . . . . . . . . . . . 5

History of Murder . . . . . . . . . . . . . . . . . . . . . . . . . 5

Historical Perspectives of the Serial Killer . . . . . . . . . . . . . . . 8

Modern Legal Perspectives/Perceptions of the Serial Killer . . . . . . . . . . 15

External Theory: Why People Become Serial Killers . . . . . . . . . . 15

Internal Theory: Why People Become Serial Killers . . . . . . . . . . 19

The 'Victim' Chooses the Profession of Serial Killer . . . . . . . . . . 23

Personal Criteria of the Professional Serial Killer: Professional
Characteristics . . . . . . . . . . . . . . . . . . . . . . . . . . 24

The Right and Justification of the Profession of Serial Killer: The Motive . . . . . . . 30

The Act in the Art of the Profession: The Mode . . . . . . . . . . . . . . 32

Perfecting the Art of the Profession: Victim Choice and Victim
Characteristics . . . . . . . . . . . . . . . . . . . . . . . . . 36

Forensic Psychology: Criminal Profiler and Criminal Profiling . . . . . . . . 38

Professional Choices: David Pelzer—A Child Called IT . . . . . . . . . . 41

Professional Choices: Solutions to the Problem . . . . . . . . . . . . . . 43

Professional Choice: Resolution to the Problem . . . . . . . . . . . . 44

**CHAPTER 3**     The Career of Ted Bundy . . . . . . . . . . 45

**CHAPTER 4**     Summary . . . . . . . . . . . . . . . . . . . 63

CHAPTER 5     Conclusion. . . . . . . . . . . . . . . . . . . . . . . . . . . . . . 66

Appendix. . . . . . . . . . . . . . . . . . . . . . . . . . . . . . . . . . . . . . . . . . 67

Glossary. . . . . . . . . . . . . . . . . . . . . . . . . . . . . . . . . . . . . . . . . . 69

Bibliography . . . . . . . . . . . . . . . . . . . . . . . . . . . . . . . . . . . . . . 71

# *Preface*

The purpose of this book is an alternate approach in the study of the serial killer. It is meant to promote another perspective of the serial killer who, in this context, raises the bar of the common killer, to that of a professional. While secretly masking their primary and true profession of a killer, these individuals cleverly portray themselves as artists of another secondary or cover profession. As they intensively study what they believe to be as, normal behavior of other worthy and comparable professionals, these killers mimic and act out the roles of physicians, lawyers, politicians, clergymen and the like; while they calculatingly sell themselves off to the unsuspecting and vulnerable, public.

This book is also written with the intent of promoting a pro-active approach to identify those children, who find themselves alone and in trouble, today and tomorrow.

# *Acknowledgements*

My sincerest thanks to my family, friends, and colleagues who gave me constant direction and support on my journey towards a better understanding of the professional serial killer.

A special thanks to Rita Majorossy who listened to my constant revelations without judgment, and, who graciously taught me patience, perseverance, and persistence. My Best Friend.

My Thanks To You All.

# 1

# *Introduction*

Historical and modern research portrays the serial killer as an individual who is a: monster, vampire, devil, lunatic, or more appropriately, insane. These labels manifested from traditional perspective, derived out of common and collective perceptions, categorizes the serial killer as: not one of us. Or is He? It is the premise of this writer that the serial killer is an ordinary but unique individual. An individual, like serial killer Ted Bundy who proclaims: "we serial killers are your sons, we are your husbands, we are everywhere." (Brown 2003, 9) The only differentiation therefore, according to Bundy, between the serial killer and the common man, is minimal. As rational and valid his proclamation may seem, it is the contention of this writer that, what really differentiates the serial killer from the everyday man, is the very reliability of Bundy's statement; it is that which makes serial killers like: Jack the Ripper, Chikatilo, Fish, Bundy, Dahmer, Gein, Gacey, and Rader so unique. It is their chosen Profession of *SERIAL KILLER*.

In order to conceptualize this premise, the writer invites the reader to think about the serial killer not as a monster or insane, but as an individual; one who has cognitively chosen his profession, one who is continually mastering the art of serial killing. And interestingly, one who in all his grandiosity of his profession, has vastly become a serious problem in our society. Consequently, in addition to viewing the serial killer in this diverse perspective, the process of understanding the problem, proactive detection of the problem and prevention of the problem before it evolves into a profession, will be discussed in forthcoming chapters.

## Background of the Problem

Since the inception of communication, historical and modern documentation on the subject of mass murderers and serial killers, has been influenced by emotion and skewed by society's immediacy of apprehension. Research clearly demonstrates the perception that: due to the impossibility of the killer being one of us, the only other recourse for rationalization of such atrocities is that the killer must be evil therefore the devil; one who not only acts possessed but has the outward appearances of being possessed; someone who is ugly and resembles the Hunchback of Notre Dame. Subsequent historical reasoning and labeling therefore, has gradually found its way into a more modern version of the plight of the serial killer, only to depict the killer as a victim of his childhood; ultimately to be declared mentally incapacitated, demented or insane. Interestingly enough, it is this emotional reasoning, passion for adjectives, and consequential labeling, we read in the headlines of the newspaper that drives the police to *quickly* apprehend the serial killer; only to quell the reader's fears of being terrorized by this monster. This process of reasoning, better known as inductive reasoning, historically has proven to be a quick but costly fix or remedy by the police; mainly because the wrong person has been unjustifiably apprehended and punished, just to appease society.

An updated, more useful technique called profiling (accomplished by means of deductive reasoning) is often used in an effort to resolve this problem in a more comprehensive and sophisticated manner for the eventual capture of the serial killer. This kind of reasoning focuses on a different perspective, (one that the writer uses in this project) of the serial killer as an indirect correlation to the victim and the crime scene. This type of rationale focuses on the behavioral characteristics of the killer in relation to the victims. The serial killer is perceived not as a monster or insane, but as a person, a human being, and as an individual who acts out of his own internal reasoning. Consequent to this actualization, this writer attempts to demonstrate that in the mind of the serial killer the subsequent and inadvertent drive to kill is simply a causality of his profession as a serial killer. Moreover, because his profession, like most individuals, is an evolutionary process, the initial enjoyment of the act develops into a process and subseqential pattern. As the killer realizes he enjoys and derives pleasure from the initial act of killing he realizes how much he likes it, and, to what extent it fulfills his need. Eventually, the killer *chooses* to make killing his profession, which in turn becomes his identity; eventually, the act of killing becomes an art form, which the serial killer continually attempts to perfect.

This study needs to be done in order to more clearly understand the serial killer as another human being. A person, who like most of us, has fantasies in childhood about what his profession in life will be; a person who develops a passion for this profession, one which he attempts to perfect over and over again, just like everyone else.

# Statement of the Problem

The perception of serial killers throughout history has been from sociological, psychological, legal, and theological perspectives. There are massive amounts of statistics, typologies, characteristics, behavioral patterns, differentiations of gender, age, sex, and race of the serial killer as a means of causational factors for serial murder. These studies result in what purports to be the "real" reasoning for the development of a serial killer. Blame therefore, is usually displaced on: the family, stress, alcoholism, psychopathology, genetics, predisposition, etc. A more popular and palatable perspective is that the serial killer was the victim of a traumatic childhood; all theories placing the child in a vulnerable role, a child who supposedly grows up to kill out of rage and retaliation. What about the perspective of the serial killer? What about his perception of his own causation as a killer and why he kills? Does he really think and believe he is a victim? Why is it that some children who suffer tremendous abuse, do not become serial killers as adults?

It is the writer's contention that this phenomenon begins to evolve in the mind of the child early on, and continues to develop at the discretion and the will of the child, throughout his lifetime. Consequently, for reasons of sheer pleasure, passion, art and subsequent professionalism, the serial killer is born. Consequently, the reason why these questions should be answered is to curtail the development of this profession from evolving further in our children.

It is therefore the contention of this writer, that the potential evolution of a serial killer can be identified, redirected, monitored, and rectified by our educational system and family system, i.e. teachers, counselors, parents and mentors to the child throughout his childhood and adolescence.

# Purpose of the Study

The purpose of this study is three-fold. First, to *understand* the mind of the serial killer; his passion for, and addiction to his profession. Second, to utilize the means of deductive reasoning as it relates to the *detection* and uniqueness of: thoughts, beliefs, and behavior patterns; as they have developed in the mind of the serial killer and, as they are evolving in the minds of the children and adolescents of today. Third, to *prevent* further evolution of serial killers by engaging the influence of teachers, parents and mentors, at an early age, in order to: learn their value systems, profile/gauge thoughts, beliefs, and behavior; teach differentiations of ideal verses actual choices in life as they relate to future dreams and fantasies of a profession.

The research objectives and the function of this study is demonstrated within the essential elements of its content. Therefore, the goal of the investigation is accomplished by embracing the collective sections of this study as they relate to: history of the problem, external and internal causation of the problem, personal criteria of the professional serial killer, right and justifications for the profession, act in the art of the profession, forensic psychology, solutions and resolutions.

All research comprises information obtained from studies, research articles, books, documentaries, interviews, and FBI profiles of serial killers.

## Theoretical Framework

Due to historical and modern theoretical misconceptions of the serial killer, focus has been placed on his maladaptive nature and irrational belief system. Subsequent blame for, even the serial killer's existence, is displaced to childhood trauma and consequent victimization. This perception is a tremendous underestimation of the serial killer.

It is the premise of this writer that the serial killer is a calculating professional; one who takes great pride in his profession, one who covets its identity and protects its exposure. Passion for an addiction to his profession drives the serial killer to raise the bar of killing to an art.

My contention is that the serial killer is a master at using society's sympathy about his victimization as a child to his benefit. In reality the serial killer sees himself, during childhood, in a situation where he has an opportunity of amusement per se; a way or means of satisfying his needs by doing whatever pleases him.

If this premise is true, then as a society we need to curtail the possibility and potentiality of future children fantasizing about and evolving into future serial killers of tomorrow.

We can accomplish this with various solutions and resolutions which include but are not limited to bringing back the family.

# 2

# *Literature Review*

## History of Murder

Since the beginning of time, history of mankind has been plagued with the atrocities of mass murder; atrocities that have been accomplished either by random or specific selection. Research demonstrates that these heinous acts touched all areas of the globe, which documentation of them, has been insurmountably accomplished in all forms and means of communication.

Historical documentation of mass murder begins, as far back as "ancient Rome, when Emperor Caligula was busily indulging his taste for torture and perversion." (Schechter and Everitt 1997, 115) During this same period of time, St. Jerome wrote about "Scottish man-eating as late as the fourteenth century." (Everitt 1993, 3) Interestingly enough some researchers pinpoint this man to exist in either the late 14th or early 15th centuries. Nevertheless, it was Sawney Bean of Scotland, who murdered to steal the money of acquaintances, only to cannibalize the flesh of his victims. In the 15th century, it was Baron Gilles de Rais of France "who may be considered to be the true 'father' of modern serial murderers." (Apsche 1993, 5) The Baron, who was born into aristocracy, murdered a minimum of "800 children during an eight year life-span." (Apsche 1993, 5) As he declared "that torturing the innocent was entirely for my own pleasure and physical delight" (Family Tree 2003), the Baron would dispatch his servants out to the countryside, to harvest children and bring them back to him for his pleasure. The 16th and 17th centuries had no mercy on future victims of mass murderers. Marie de Brinvilliers of France murdered members of her family in order to benefit from a wealthy inheritance. Catherine Montvoisin also of France arranged for the murder of several hundred infants for the purpose of reimbursement. According to research it was Jack the Ripper of 19th century England, who was the first serial *sex-killer*. This man, who to this day, has yet to be identified, terrorized London by: slaughtering five street walkers by slashing their abdomens, stabbing their genitalia, and disemboweling them. According to written reports by a constable, one of the Ripper's victims had "been gutted like a pig in the market, with her entrails flung in a heap about her neck." (Newton 2000, 113) More recently, in the 20th century, surveys have continued to demonstrate the prevalence of mass murder and serial killings in other countries. One of the most notorious was Pietro Pacciani of Italy, who sexually mutilated his victims, as a *trademark* of the killer; he mailed the police an envelope, inside "they found a portion of [a] murdered woman's genitalia." (Newton 2000, 159) Paul Ogorzov of Germany, a railroad worker, beat and strangled eight women to death, raping most of these women before they died. In Japan, Okubo Kiyoshi attacked 127 women (other reports say more like 150), raped twelve or more, and murdered eight of them. Anatoly Onoprienko, better known as the Terminator, was born in the Ukraine; as a serial killer Onoprienko attacked and slaughtered entire families at one time. The last count for this killer was fifty-two victims, mostly immediate members of each family. Prussia was not immune from the ravages of the serial killer. Carl Panzram rented a yacht and lured several sailors to the vessel with the offer of liquor; he then murdered them and dumped their bodies into the ocean. "In Portuguese, West Africa, Panzram hired eight blacks to help him hunt crocodiles, then killed them, sodomized their corpses, and fed them to the hungry reptiles." (Newton 2000, 181) When asked why he did this he replied "for the fun it gave me." (Newton 2000, 181) Russia was no exception to the atrocities of the mass murderer; the 'Rostov Ripper,' Andrei Chikatilo was declared the most monstrous of Russian serial sex-killers. The movie *Citizen X* expertly and ingeniously portrayed Chikatilo as a Russian madman who preyed on fifty two young women and children. A killer who confessed to raping and stabbing his victims; some who had their tongues chewed off, others who had been disemboweled. At times he would go further and drink the blood of the corpses, and did admit to chewing on their internal organs. Additional countries such as Holland's Sjef Rijke killed all of his fiancés with rat poison, only to proclaim the enjoyment he felt as he watched all of them suffer. Spain's Jose Antoinio Rodriques Vega killed elderly women on his rampage; after strangling his victims and raping their corpses, Vega would put their bodies back to bed. In the 21st century the most bizarre case of international murderers, is the case of Armin Meiwes of Germany. Meiwes confessed that he placed an ad on the internet "seeking a young man for slaughter and consumption ... he got more than 400 responses." (Alleged Cannibal 2003) Upon apprehension, Meiwes boasted that he froze some flesh and burned the rest in his garden.

On a national level, research further demonstrates that the United States has historically been plagued by the atrocities of serial murders and their killers. In the late 18th century recorded massacres by the Harper Brothers who terrorized those victims traveling across the Wilderness Trail, by disemboweling them and throwing their corpses into the nearby rivers and lakes. In the 19th century Thomas Piper, Church Sexton in Boston, was one of many serial murderers who was convicted of killing three women and the torture and slaying of several children in his neighborhood. In the 20th century, the United States had witnessed a continuous increase in mass murder and serial killing. This upsurge was initiated in the early 1900's by none other than Albert Fish, nicknamed the Werewolf of Wisteria. This killer who reportedly "enjoyed dancing naked in the full moon" (Family Tree, 2003) proclaimed that he was "ordered by God to castrate young boys, he impartially molested children of both sexes ... from New York to Wyoming he declared his own tally of victims [close] to 400." (Albert Fish, 2004) In the 1920's Leonard Nelson, a bible preaching man, strangled and raped his landladies from one coast to another. The 1930's was plagued by the Mad Butcher of Cleveland, Ohio who dissected sixteen of his victims so professionally, that Elliott Ness could not find ten of the skulls. Edward Gein was the notorious killer between the 1940's and 1950's. Gein, who was the subject of several motion pictures, most recently, *Silence of the Lambs*, decided to be a part time transsexual by cutting the flesh from his deceased female victims, and sewing it into a body shape that he would wrap around his own. In the 1960's Edmund Kemper initiated his killing spree with shooting his grandmother then his grandfather. Later on, after killing several female hitchhikers and dismembering their bodies, Kemper decided to kill his mother who historically "berated him steadily, saying that he was responsible for her dating problems." (The Case 2004) David Berkowitz better known in the 1970's as the Son of Sam preyed on female victims in the night in New York. The terror and carnage of murder lasted thirteen months by shooting several victims in the head; Berkowitz was also responsible for setting 300 fires in the City of New York. Interestingly enough, Berkowitz claimed that he was not alone and that he was part of a cult and a spin off of the Scientology Movement, which was linked to Charles Manson. "I'm the most cold blooded son-of-a-bitch you'll ever meet ... I just like to kill" (Psychopaths? 2003) was Ted Bundy's motto. From the 1970's and into the 1980's Bundy took great pleasure in abducting and murdering female college students in Washington, Colorado and Utah. While in Florida, Bundy broke into the Chi Omega Sorority house on the Florida State University Campus and proceeded to attack and rape the coeds as he ran room to room; he killed two of the coeds in the house and another as he returned to his apartment. It was John Wayne Gacey who in the 1980's "liked to dress as a clown for charity events in Des Plaines, Iowa." (Innes 2003, 212) Twenty-nine decomposed corpses were found in the crawl spaces of Gacey's home; after he had spent several hours "sodomizing and torturing [young men] before committing the final outrage—the rope trick." (Schechter 2003, 196) Jeffrey Dahmer was better known as the "most notorious sex murderer in popular culture." (Dahmer Case 2003) In the 1990's Dahmer eventually confessed to the murder and partial cannibalization of seventeen male victims. The police later realized that Dahmer was attempting to turn some of his favored victims into zombies by "drilling holes in the selected victims' skull, then dribbling caustic liquids into the wounds in an effort to destroy the victim's conscious will." (Jeffrey Dahmer 2004) It was Dennis Rader "the self named BTK ('for bind, torture, kill') … who was the only criminal who meets criteria … as mass murderer, a serial killer, and domestic terrorist." (Beattie 2005, xi)

## Historical Perspectives of the Serial Killer

Historical documented research has shown that in order to answer the question of who could possibly accomplish these atrocities, with the politically correct and accepted rationalization "to affirm that mass murderers and serial killers [were] neither civilized nor really human … to perceive them as belonging to the realm of the other." (Grixti 1995, 88) These speculations further resolved that, characterlogically, these heinous acts had to be accomplished by one who is "less than human." (Grixti 1995, 88) It was with this logic and reasoning that those who historically committed these atrocities were to be labeled as monsters, vampires, beasts, fiends, lunatics, and demons. Newspapers for example "described such criminals in supernatural terms: 'murder fiends' or 'bloodthirsty monsters' or devils in 'human shape'" (Schechter 2003, 3) who were obviously possessed by evil. Interestingly enough, the inference of lunacy and the inductive reasoning used to label these originators of atrocity was developed only "from observation" (Inductive and Deductive, 2004) speculation, gut feeling, and hearsay. Intriguingly, in reality, society has historically had individuals such as: "Ludwig van Beethoven, Robert Schuman, Peter Ilich Tchaikovsky" (Szegedy-Mazak 2003, 46) as well as "Lord Byron, Edgar Allan Poe, and Vincent Van Gogh," (Kluger-Song 2002, 43) among several others who really were mad or deranged.

In order to rid all of these possessed, insane, and deranged individuals from their demons and, the "radical evil, like the malevolence of tyrants and mass murderers," (Begley 2001, 37) punishments so called remedies or treatments, were established.

The goal of these remedies, among others, was to either: excise the madness from the brain of the individual or, to banish by exorcism, the devil out of the person. Consequently, treatment for these individuals, perceived and labeled as insane or monsters, was no less than harsh and extreme, which was swift and effective, in the minds of those vulnerable citizens, who may become future prey to the atrocities of the serial murderer. Treatment for individuals such as these dates back to the "stone age ... some skulls from that period recovered in Europe and South America show evidence of an operation called trephination ... in which a stone instrument, or trephine, was used to cut away a circular section of the skull." (Comer 2002, 9) Illustration one depicts the expelling of evil spirits by trephination "possibly for the purpose of releasing evil spirits and curing mental dysfunction." (Comer 2002, 9) Later on, the Egyptians, Chinese, and Hebrews treated this plight of evil by exorcism conducted by a Shaman. Greek and Roman treatments, specifically Hippocrates, and Aretaeus, used vegetable diets, exercise, celibacy, bleeding, music, massages, and baths (respectively) to calm internal causes of mental disorders. The Middle Ages was fraught with conflict, "deviant behavior, especially psychological dysfunction, was seen as evidence of Satan's influence." (Comer 2002, 10) Treatment during this time period was the revival of exorcism conducted by the clergy, as depicted in Illustration two where we see a member of the clergy exorcising evil from a possessed woman. It was during this time that "tens of thousands of people, mostly women, were thought to have made a pact with the devil." (Comer 2002, 11) In Illustration three we see a priest removing the stone of madness from a man's head. Another treatment, as seen in Illustration four, depicts a condemned woman by dunking her repeatedly until she confesses to witchery. During the early Renaissance to early mid 16th century the treatment for those wretched individuals was less harsh, families were now caring for these people while religious shrines were erected devoted to "the humane and loving treatment of people with mental disorders." (Comer 2002, 12) By late mid 16th century to the 18th century, the loving care and treatment of the insane was fraught with overcrowding, with an increasing number of homes incapable of caring for the more severely disturbed. Consequently, in order to accommodate this problem "the municipal authorities converted hospitals and monasteries into asylums." (Comer 2002, 12) Illustration five depicts the bedlam at one hospital due to the chaos. Several hospitals including the Lunatics' Tower in Vienna and the La Bicetre in Paris were among the most notorious asylums of their time; known for their atrocious and inhumane treatment by the attendants for controlling the insane, with the use of the "crib" as seen in Illustration six. Ironically, if one compares these atrocities which the attendants inflicted on the vulnerable masses, to those atrocities committed by mass murderers, which they also inflicted on the vulnerable masses, one would soon realize an emerging similarity between the two groups. "During the 17th and 18th centuries hospital care of the sick of all kinds … fell to the lowest ebb in history … institutions and care for the insane, not only shared in this decadence, but were its worst feature." (Asylums, 2004) By the 19th century, reform was reoccurring for the mentally insane; this time the focus of these institutions was the use of "moral guidance and humane and respectful techniques." (Comer 2002, 13) Benjamin Rush a renowned physician in the service of Pennsylvania Hospital ordered the hiring of intellectual and rational attendants who would treat the patients with dignity and respect. Rush further ordered the attendants and other physicians to be empathetic while counseling the patients in order to perceive their plight as not lunacy but a manifestation of stress. Interestingly, the painting by George Bellows named "Dance in the Madhouse" as depicted in Illustration seven shows the moral treatment of the patients as they dance together at the "Lunatic Ball." (Comer 2002, 13) Subsequent decline of the moral treatment movement evolved into a "new wave of prejudice against people with mental disorders." (Comer 2002, 14) By the early 20th century a shift of perspective with consequential labeling evolved. It was during this time that the terms syndrome and symptoms were used to describe what once was labeled lunacy. Treatments during this time period were now in the hands of the researchers, neurologists, physicians, and psychiatrists. Researcher, Emil Kraepelin was the first to "measure the effects of various drugs on behavior." (Comer, 2002, 15) Neurologist Richard VanKrafft-Ebing injected, better known as vaccinated, patients from syphilis, "physicians tried tooth extraction, tonsillectomy, hydrotherapy, (alternating hot and cold baths), and lobotomy, a surgical severing of certain nerve fibers in the brain." (Comer 2002, 16) Physician, Anton Mesmer used hypnosis, while two additional physicians Hippolyte-Marie Bernheim and Ambroise-Auguste Liebault established hypnotic suggestion as the answer; Josef Bruer and Sigmund Freud, both physicians treated their mentally ill patients with psycho-analysis. Currently, the 21st century has seen a rise in the use of psychotropic medications "drugs that primarily affect the brain, and alleviate many symptoms of mental dysfunction." (Comer 2002, 17) Outpatient counseling is an additional option of treatment for those with severe psychological problems as well as those with milder cases. At present when "severely *impaired* people do need institutionalization they are usually given short-term hospitalization." (Comer 2002, 18) Today treatment approaches include but are not limited to: "behavioral, cognitive, humanistic-existential, and socio-cultural schools of thought." (Comer 2002, 20)

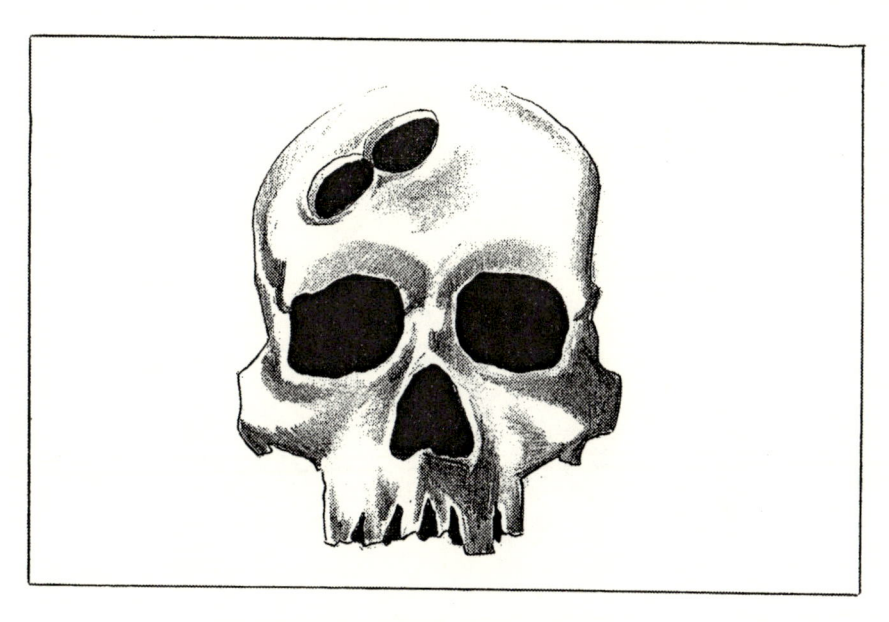

Expelling Evil Spirits by Trephination

Members of the Clergy Exorcising Evil From a Possessed Woman

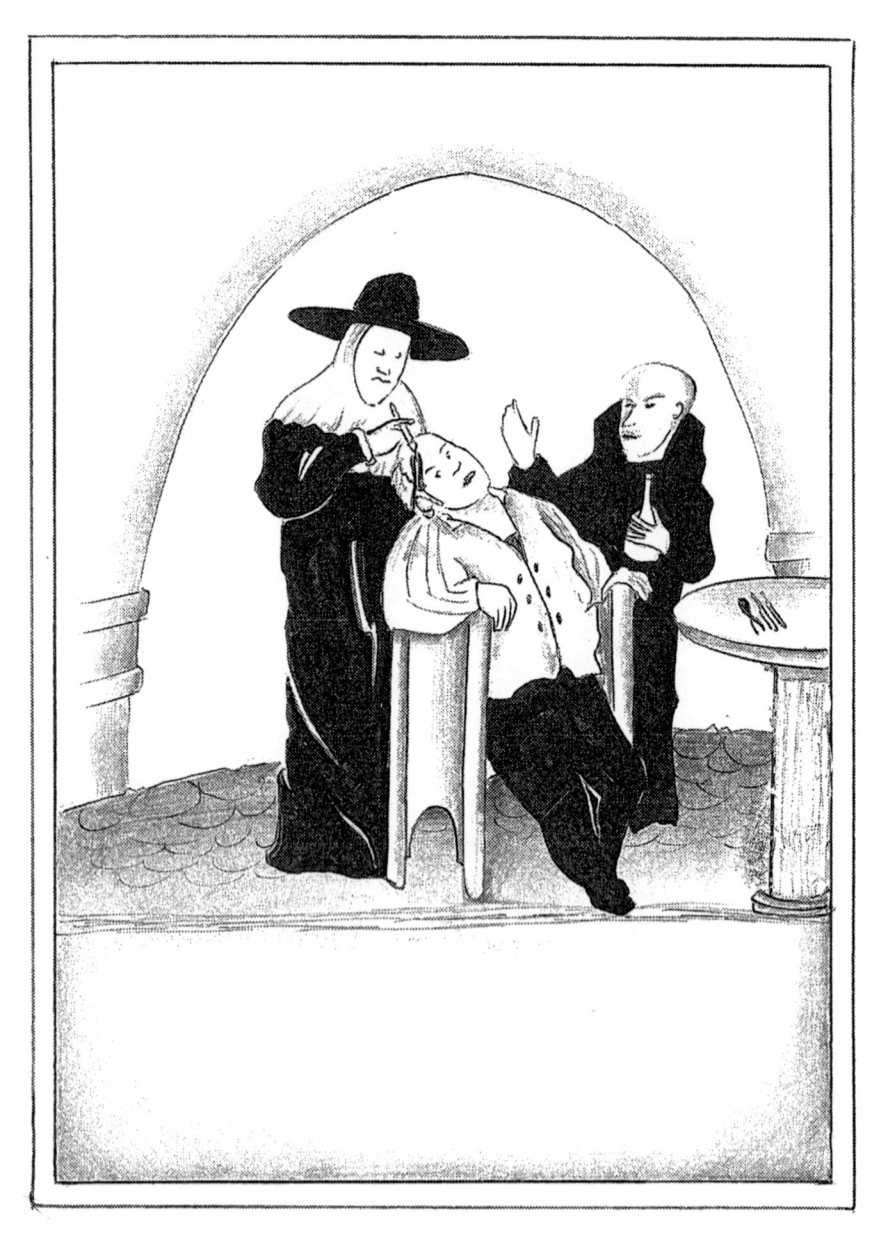

A Priest Removing the Stone of Madness From a Man's Head

A Condemned Woman Being Dunked

Bedlam at a Hospital in the 18th Century

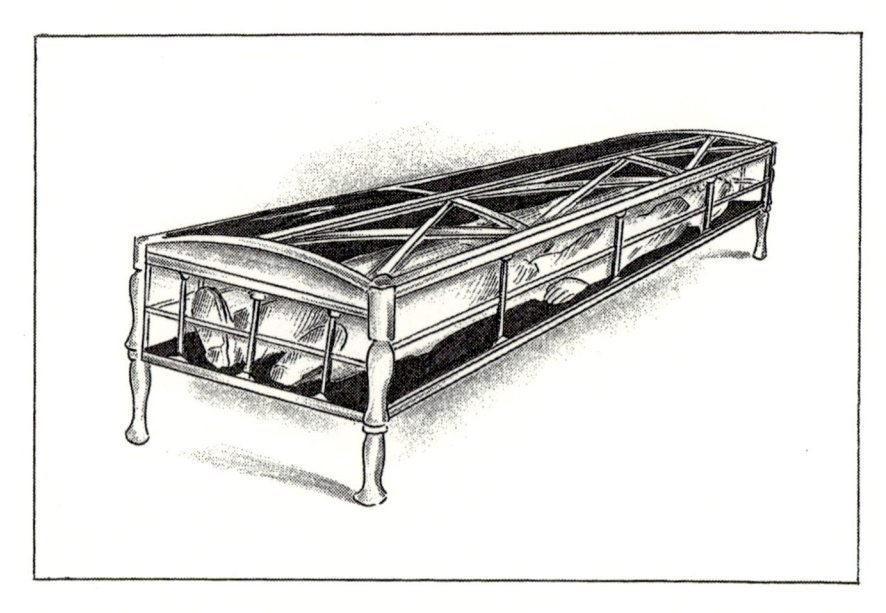

The "Crib"

Dance at the "Lunatic Ball"

# Modern Legal Perspectives/Perceptions of the Serial Killer

Interestingly, perspectives of treatment developed and historical perceptions in regard to labeling evolved for the mass murderer from: monster, vampire, beast, fiend, lunatic to insane. Current judicial and social trends of today, now perceive and do declare, these killers or monsters, as *sane.* Treatment for these serial killers and mass murderers has recently changed from institutionalization for the criminally insane, to incarceration for life, without the possibility of parole, or death. Surprisingly, the death penalty has been waived for some, such as Charles Manson, while the insanity plea was successful for Ed Gein, Albert Fish was not so lucky, although the "jury found him 'insane' … he deserved to die anyway." (Are they insane 2003) Roger Shawcross claimed insanity, but "declared sane and given 250 years in prison." (Olshaker and Klein 1992) Andrei Chikatilo was executed with a shot to the back of his head. Wayne Gacey also attempted to plead insanity but was sentenced to death. Jeffrey Dahmer was sentenced to life without parole, but was bludgeoned to death by another inmate. Ted Bundy was sentenced to death after he attempted to try his own case. He was sentenced to be executed in Florida's electric chair.

Interestingly enough, it is easy to understand how their treatment was directly related to how all of these mass murderers and serial killers were perceived.

# External Theory: Why People Become Serial Killers

*Perception is in the eye of the beholder.*

—Bonnie Rippo 2006

Even though these serial killers and mass murderers have been captured, incarcerated or executed, speculation continues to remain about why people commit these atrocities, by murdering the vulnerable. Historical perceptions, derived from Sociological, Theological, Philosophical, Psychological, and Biological perspectives, indicate that the first documented case of these killers was initiated and generated from the prehistoric perspective. These societies viewed the maladaptive behavior as the "work of evil spirits." (Comer 2002,) "The ancient Greek philosophers and physicians looked deeply into the question of emotions, their cause and where they might originate in the human body." (Innes 2003, 9) Hippocrates, a well respected physician of that era (460-377 B.C.), surmised that the problem was not one of demonology but that of: disease in the body; the physician "Aretaeus suggested that this behavior could also be caused by emotional problems." (Comer 2002, 10)

"The Gospel of St. Matthew in the bible refers to two persons possessed with devils who were exceedingly fierce ... when Christ [cast] them out they ... immediately entered the bodies of swine." (Hickey 2002, 37) The religious order of the Middle Ages in Europe decidedly took over control of all education, "which was far removed from the liturgical and doctrinal controversies of the elite;" (Cummingham 1993) only to proclaim causation for abnormality of behavior was *not* caused by physiological complications but rather as a "conflict between good and evil. God and the devil, deviant behavior ... was seen as evidence of Satan's influence." (Comer 2002, 10) As demonology causation dwindled, the rejuvenation of medical causation was rekindled in the early Renaissance eras; only this time the perspective focused on "natural causes, such as 'blow to the head'" (Comer 2002, 11) as speculation for lunacy and madness. Later on, it was the research of German Doctor Johan Weyer who speculated that the etiology of this behavior was directly related to the mind, and that it was just as vulnerable to disease as that of the body. It was also during this time period (16th century) that physiognomy was popular, the "ideas ... that it was possible to determine that nature of a person by his external features, such as the forehead, mouth, eyes, teeth, nose, or hair." (Innes 2003, 10) This perspective put a different slant on causation of behavior. The combination of the physical, and more recently, the psychological perspective of behavior, incorporated the study of phrenology (17th century) to resolve the issue of etiology of abnormal behavior. Phrenology, the study of the surface of the brain, popularized by Franz Joseph Gall (ending 18th century) concluded that the "brain was made up of thirty-three organs whose position and developed size could be discovered by feeling external bumps on the cranium;" (Innes 2003, 11) inferring cranial structural configuration as behavioral causation for abnormal behavior. Philippe Pinel a well respected physician in Paris in the 18th century, was most influential in turning the perspectives of abnormality and accompanying behavior around to focus on the individual as being *sick*. Due to the decline of this premise, "a new wave of prejudice against people with mental disorders evolved ... [they were now viewed as] strange and dangerous." (Comer 2002, 14) In order to quell the anxiety of the 19th century collective society, the physician, Alphonse Bertillon, popularized the study of Anthropometry, the "taking of physical measurements of human beings, and particularly their skeletons, in the hope of supporting—or refuting—Darwin's theories about evolution of humankind." (Innes 2003, 14) Interestingly enough, according to ancient custom, Darwin may have been influenced by the 'Atavistic' perspective: an "ancestral trait that reappears in modern life" (Schechter 2003, 247) that predestined those who commit atrocities; who seem like creatures from a primitive age when cannibalism, human sacrifice, and similar barbaric practices were rife in the world." (Schechter 2003, 247) In addition, the term 'natural born' killers was coined by Phrenologist, Cesare Lombroso during this time. "The phrase 'the bad seed' ... [meaning] that some people are just born evil," (Schechter 2003, 255) was a prevalent perspective of the 20th century, starting with "the somatogenic perspective, the view that abnormal psychological functioning has physical causes." (Comer 2002, 15) Surprisingly, "scientific discoveries seem to confirm that severely antisocial personalities are at least partly the product of genetic factors," (Schechter 2003 256) called the *'mean gene.'* This perspective, also dictates that this gene is also shared by the parents who, inadvertently reinforce its predisposition as a result of their own maladaptive and abnormal behavior indicative of serial killers is caused by: genetic differences, particularly in the frontal lobe of the brain. These studies have developed "enough data to implicate the frontal brain in the genesis of dissocial and antisocial personalities." (Rutigliano, nd) It seems that the "serial killer is doomed to repeat a never-ending cycle of compulsion and death." (Simon 2000) In addition, studies have further shown "that the nervous system of [the serial killer] is markedly different ... indicating low arousal levels ... [causing] impulsiveness and thrill seeking." (Psychopaths? 2003) In the late 20th century and present 21st century further studies have been conducted with the intent on finding physiological causational factors that drive the serial killer to commit murder. One study suggested that these killers possess one X chromosome and two Y chromosomes; however, the evidence of reality and validity is minimal. Another study suggested that high testosterone levels combined with low levels of serotonin may be responsible for abnormal behavior. Studies involving the research of heavy metals such as: manganese, lead, calcimine and copper have shown up in toxicology testing of some serial killers. Other research has shown brain defects. While additional studies have realized parts of the brain of these violent offenders, such as the limbic brain or the temporal lobe, have had lesions or had been damaged in some way. Interestingly, "researcher Dominique La Pierre believes that the 'prefrontal cortex' and area of the brain involved in long term planning and judgment does not function properly in [serial killers]." (Natural Born 2003) Another study by Pavlos Hatzltaskos reported that a large percentage of the inmates on death row had suffered head injuries, "70% ... [of these] patients developed aggressive tendencies ... some of these brain injuries are accidental, but many of them were inflicted during childhood." (Natural Born 2003)

The "Psychogenic Perspective, the view that the chief causes of abnormal functioning are psychological," (Comer 2002, 15) are significantly related to the emotional and mental aspects of the individual. The late 20th and early 21st centuries have elicited an impressive upsurge in the psychological study of abnormal or deviant behavior. A recent study on "The Effects of Partner Violence and Physical Child Abuse or Child Behavior" by Salzinger, Feldman and Ng-Mak (2002, 43) clearly demonstrates "that high levels of family stress, caretaker distress and violence between the two parents increases the likelihood of: not only child abuse but poor child behavioral outcome." Consequent to this outcome, extreme deviance from the normally accepted childhood behavior can evolve into what the Diagnostic Manual of Mental Disorders use to diagnose as psychopathic or sociopathic personality disorders. Psychopaths are described as those "individuals who lack remorse and guilt, they are selfish individuals who only look out for themselves; they are cunning and resourceful, often leaving behind a trail of individuals whom they have victimized." (Psychopathy 2004) An impressive article *Psychopathy: An Evolutionary Perspective* proposes that the "psychopath is genetically predisposed to the disorder, in most cases, a warm and caring family environment can inhibit the development of psychopathy." (Psychopathy 2004) The sociopaths are individuals who possess maladaptive social behavior: very cunning and highly manipulative, but without any sense of guilt or remorse for victims they leave behind. Both of these terms have been streamlined into present day diagnosis of Antisocial Personality Disorder within the context of the 2002 Diagnostic Manual of Mental Disorders (DSM-IV-TR, Revised, 2002) The "essential feature of the Antisocial Personality Disorder is a pervasive pattern of disregard for, and violation of, the rights of others that begin in childhood or early adolescence and continue into adulthood." (DSM-IV-TR 2002) Conclusions involving psychological perspectives for causation of abnormal violent behavior indicate in some studies, that childhood fantasies evolve into the projection of anger, or transfer aggression, i.e.: taking out anger, rage, or aggression on an individual that represent the actual individual the killer is really angry with. In his article on psychopathic sexual sadists, Geberth demonstrates and confirms that childhood fantasies of aggression evolve into adult obsessive-compulsive fantasies directed towards those "whom they experience as objects" (Geberth 1995) but, according to Freud, subconscious representations of whom they really want to control and destroy.

According to Dr. Robert Keppel, Chief Criminal Investigator for the Washington State Attorney General's Office, he agrees with the transfer aggression perspective. Dr. Keppel states that "anyone who investigates sex crimes knows that even the most minor of sex offenses directed against a victim is driven by the offender's anger and his needs to express it through control." (Keppel 1997, 87)

Interestingly, Dr. Stanton Samenow, a world renowned expert on the mind of the serial killer refutes the idea and perception of causality on: "society, broken homes, alcoholism, television violence, and unemployment," (Ramsland 2002, 57) as the only forces responsible for the development of a serial killer. Dr. Samenow further "insists that, the criminal's way of thinking is vastly different and that the 'errors in logic' derive from a pattern of behavior that began in childhood." (Ramsland 2002, 57)

# Internal Theory: Why People Become Serial Killers

*"Your thoughts create your destiny"*

—Suze Orman (Cook 1993, 40)

It is the premise and contention of this writer that: personal or internal causation of why an individual becomes a serial killer is because he basically, *wants to be one.* Therefore, he thinks of it as his **Profession.**

Although this perspective may seem to be a rather simplistic rationale for causation, it is one that is logical and possibly more palatable than other perspectives previously reviewed. In order to journey down this path the writer does not dismiss the external influences that exist in the life of a child, but rather proposes that the child willfully takes a detour down a side street in order to fulfill a fantasy or, to make a dream come true. That dream is to: become someone great, someone who, like the average man, wants notoriety for his talent or artwork in his profession as serial killer. In order to set the stage for this perspective, it is important for the reader to understand that, the stage that is set, is through the minds eye of the child as he evolves into a professional serial killer. This stage or platform in which the child's frame of reference is constructed is a reference point: a fundamental set of events or circumstances when the child's impetus of thought is first initiated. In order to clearly understand this perspective, it is important that we realize that this child views his experiences, while on his childhood 'stage', as an opportunity; one in which he uses to energize and give impetus to, his future profession of serial killer. Let us take for example the childhood of serial killer Carl Panzram; a 20th century reform school was his stage. "The stories of sadistic guards and medieval punishments ... [encouraged his decision to] rob, burn, destroy and kill everywhere I went and everybody I could as long as I lived." (Childhood Events 2003) The reference point for Albert Fish was no less influential, while in a Washington, D.C. orphanage, Fish related that "I saw so many boys whipped, it took root in my head." (Childhood Events 2003) Charlie Manson claimed his stage was at a reform school where he "was raped and beaten by other prisoners when he was fourteen." (Childhood Events 2003) David Berkowitz realized that he had been adopted; the stage was set for him when he found his biological mother who "brushed him off." (Childhood Events 2003) Edmund Kemper, a child who quickly grew extremely tall, was "banished to a makeshift basement bedroom [by his mother] fearing he might try to molest his sisters ... afterwards he dismembered two family cats and played 'gas chamber' with his sisters." (The Case 2004) Kemper "told his sister that he wanted to kiss his second grade teacher, but 'if I kiss her I would have to kill her first.'" (Child Abuse 2003) Jeffrey Dahmer witnessed severe arguments between his mother and father which Jeffrey concluded that home was not a safe environment. "By the age of ten, Dahmer was experimenting with dead animals." (Jeffrey Dahmer, 2004) "At the age of thirteen he wanted to hypnotize and cast a spell over a girl, 'so I could control her entirely.'" (Dahmer Case 2003) Ted Bundy and his mother lived with his maternal grandparents; his grandfather was beating his grandmother and sadistically kicked dogs, while throwing cats around. "Barely three, Ted's fifteen year old aunt awoke to find him lifting her blankets, slipping butcher knives into the bed bedside her, 'he just stood there and grinned,' she recalled." (Newton 2000, 242)

At first glance, sympathy and empathy for these children are normal reactions to such atrocities experienced on the stage of life. However, at a second glance, it becomes clear that their perceptions of their experiences were catalysts for not only early violence and trauma, but for continued future upgrading of their atrocities. Thought patterns for these children included more sophisticated, as well as, graduated fantasies about who, what, where, when, and how they would commit the next act, that would proudly feed their ego. While concurrently believing they are the best and the greatest of their kind, these beliefs gradually advanced into a value system of righteousness. Interestingly enough, this concept is not too far off the track of anyone for that matter, who knows what he wants to be at a very early age. Is it not a normal practice that a child who does know, or one who has an inkling at an early age of the type of profession he wants to go into, starts working towards that goal early on? If we can view this perspective through the eyes of children such as Dahmer, Bundy, Manson, Fish, etc. it becomes evident that they were cognitively evolving into serial killers, by pruning themselves into this profession along the way. Surprisingly, even though their value system remains a "fundamental part of the person [they] are," (Corey and Corey 2002, 79) these children calculatingly develop a mindset, or thought process pattern, that justifies their harm to others, animals, etc. Comparatively speaking, at a closer look, the attitude, drive, ambition and passion one child has to attain his goal of a profession is, in actuality, no different from another. The question is what profession? In the mind of the evolving and developing serial killer he has to learn, or develop a way, in which to conceal who he really is. Careful not to divulge true "concealed values" (Corey and Corey 2002, 79) to the public this, now adolescent, has learned to express socially acceptable values only to use these as tools and implements in his arsenal of cunning and deception. Interestingly, one could easily argue that, most individuals have two sides to them; even Carl Jung, the founder of Analytical Psychology, proposed that everyone has a "persona, the way in which we represent ourselves to the outside world and a shadow, the thing a person has no wish to be." (Fontana 1994, 36) While the adolescent is getting on the job training, like several of us have been known to experience, those who strive to find a mentor in the profession usually finds one. In the case of the budding serial killer, he clearly intends to seek out a mentor who he worships as a hero in the field of *murder*, one who he can emulate and maybe capture direction from. The dream of finding the perfect mentor in life is, for anyone, a dream or fantasy come true; for the developing serial killer, it would be someone like Charlie Manson. A person that a teenage can idolize and worship as his hero; one who he identifies with, and strives to become a "killing machine [like him, only to] create another masterpiece of terror." (Brown 2003, 136) Interestingly, Lee Malvo, the fourteen year old boy who was abandoned in Antigua by his mother, found John Muhammad as his mentor. By the time he had found him though, Lee had already been "[talking] about killing people." (Peraino and Thomas 2003) Together they went on a killing spree in Virginia, only to be captured and incarcerated. "Children [do] decide who they want to be like and in what ways." (Samenow 1984, 42)

Rightfully so, it is a fact, that most of these young men have been abused, neglected or abandoned in some way, during their childhood. In reality, statistics show that the *highest* percentages of male offenders, who experienced forms of traumatization as children, were due to: rejection 48%; unstable home 37%; physical abuse 35% and mental and emotional abuse 34%, with a norm of 62.

Ironically, the phrase, I am the person I am today because of my past, is a thought and premise for several other victims of child abuse, who have chosen different professions. However, being a victim is an *absolute*, for the now novice, serial killer protégé. While this perspective becomes his persona, it eventually evolves into the trademark of his identity; one that allows him the opportunity of *acting* like a victim. Interestingly enough, professional actors who have actually portrayed serial killers in movies, such as Anthony Hopkins in *Silence of the Lambs*, or Anthony Perkins who played Norman Bates in *Psycho*, dissolve themselves into the character, only to play their roles as well as the serial killer plays his. Even though the two professions are morally and legally different, they are similar professions, in the respect that both leading characters are playing their given roles, *superbly.* "Serial killers are actors with a natural penchant for performance … Henry Lee Lucas described being a serial killer as 'being like a movie star' you're just playing a part." (Scott 2003) John Wayne Gacey dressed up in a clown costume, and was also a leader in his community. The Zodiac Killer dressed up in an executioners costume; while Ted Bundy, a once most effective crises counselor, told the judge at his trial "I'm disguised as an attorney today … Berkowitz 'the Son of Sam' enjoyed dressing as a police officer." (Scott 2003) Jeffrey Dahmer effectively played the role of a porn photographer; Ted Bundy lured young women to kill by pretending he had a broken arm or leg. While the mask of deception takes ingenuity, this role for the new upcoming serial killer is an additional foundation or stage on which to commit murder. In order to reinforce this perception, Jeffrey Dahmer stated that "he was born with a 'part missing' … Bundy [claimed] 'pornography made him do it' … Panzram swore 'prison turned him into a monster' … Bobby Joe Long [said] a 'motorcycle accident made him hypersexual [and into] a lust killer.'" (Scott 2003) Albert Fish stated, "I have no particular desire to live, I have no particular desire to be killed. It is a matter of indifference to me. I do not think I am altogether right." (Brown 2003, 166) Albert De Salvo stated that "society, right from the very beginning started to make me an animal … that's why I started killing." (Brown 2003, 143) Arthur Gary Bishop confessed "with great sadness and remorse, I realize that I allowed myself to be misled by Satan … [David Berkowitz said] 'I must slay a woman for revenge purposes to get back at them for all the suffering they caused me.'" (Brown 2003, 39) "I was following God's order," (Brown 2003, 17) was Joseph Kallinger's excuse for murder. While his acting ability and deceptive nature prompts the further development of his masquerade, the junior killer masters the sobering portrayal of his role as a *victim.* Subsequently, his façade becomes a means to an end for the ongoing progression into the profession of serial killer.

# The 'Victim' Chooses the Profession of Serial Killer

*"When the Victim Comes Knocking"*

—Bonnie Rippo 2006

As public justification for his actions prevail, the upcoming serial killer continues to refine his private more personal hidden agenda for killing. He accomplishes this by narcissistically elevating the *act* of killing, to a professional level. In his mind, he now has internalized his actions as that of a profession; equal to and, no less than, the status of any other professional. His profession therefore is now perceived as on the same plateau, as other professionals, whose profession's obligate them to kill for sport or as part of their job such as: a rancher, farmer, hunter or fisherman. In order to meet the demands of his own personal criteria of his profession, the now seasoned serial killer has to strengthen and embellish his need for power. He accomplishes this by enjoying public notoriety. David Berkowitz stated, "I believe they are rooting for me ... and was thrilled to hear his co-workers at the post office chat about the 'Son of Sam.'" (Social Evils 2003). Gacey "treasured his scrapbook of all the press he received ... Jeffrey Dahmer's trial has an air of a movie premier, complete with local celebrities, and groupies who hounded for autographs." (Social Evils 2003) In addition to this external reinforcement of power, the elation they receive by killing, feeds their internal desire to possess superhuman power they enjoy comparing to God. Ted Bundy remarked that as "you feel the last breath leaving their body ... you're looking into their eyes. A person in that situation is God." (Brown 2003, 53). Charlie Manson stated "look down on me; you will see a fool. Look up at me; you will see your Lord." (Brown 2003, 11)

Emotional self conditioning, for the purpose of feeling no pain is a hallmark of the serial killers' profession. As he comparatively chooses his prey, so does the hunter or cattleman who chooses an animal to be destroyed, for whatever reason. Emotion for the killer, at all costs, is expertly controlled; therefore feelings of guilt, remorse and empathy play a minimal role in the serial killer's profession. For someone such as Ted Bundy, guilt was "an illusion ... it's a kind of social control mechanism—and it's very unhealthy ... there are much better ways to control our behavior than that rather extraordinary use of guilt." (Hare 1999, 41) According to "Mike Rustigan, Professor of Criminology at San Francisco State University ... [serial killers] 'have no guilt, no remorse and have an attitude of total disdain for their victims.'" (Serial Killers, 2004) Bundy, who disagrees with professor Rustigan stated "alcoholics who I've known suffer a great deal of remorse. That doesn't stop them from drinking. [Interestingly] the only remorse Ted ever felt was over being caught." (Keppel 1995, 314) Lack of empathy, or the non-existence of it for the serial killer, is an additional and an essential emotion to control. Edmund Kemper stated "I am sorry to *sound* so cold about this, but what I needed to have was a particular experience with a person, and to possess them in this way, I had to evict them from their bodies." (Simon 2004, 7) It is because of their lack of remorse, the serial killer can perform atrocities to human beings as a matter of course throughout his professional life. "For example, they can torture and mutilate their victims with about the same sense of concern that we feel when we carve a turkey for Thanksgiving dinner." (Hare 1999, 45) Nevertheless, the serial killer takes great pride in continually upgrading his skills, in the area of his profession. His goal then becomes raising the bar of his profession to the level of an art form. Edmund Kemper confessed that "in the course of his murders there was always [something] … that he felt could have been more perfect … imperfection … pushed him to kill the next time … the act … was never as good as the fantasy." (The Case 2004)

The unequivocal bottom line for the now well seasoned professional killer is that his profession feeds his ego only to fuel the pleasure he derives from his craft. It is this emotional, feeding and refueling process that constantly enamors the serial killer to kill, with the intensity of the predator that he is; only to nourish his instinctual drives that Freud so elaborately defined, as the ID. Therefore, it is the premise of this writer that the reason the serial killer does kill is simply because **HE LIKES IT!** Ted Bundy boasted "I just like to kill, I wanted to kill." (Psychopaths? 2003) Vincent Verzeni stated, "I had unspeakable delight in strangling women … it satisfied me to seize the woman by the neck and suck their blood." (Brown 2003, 103) Jeffrey Dahmer claimed "I bite … [and that] eating his victims made him feel closer to them." (Brown 2003, 116) John Christie claimed that "I remember as I gazed down at the still form of my first victim, experiencing a strange and peaceful thrill." (Brown 2003, 135) Susan Atkins related the "more you do it, the better you like it." (Brown 2003, 146)

# Personal Criteria of the Professional Serial Killer: Professional Characteristics

*"I am the master of my fate, I am the captain of my soul"*

—William Henley (Invictus 2004, 1)

As a professional, the serial killer takes pride in the work that he does, he considers his profession one that he not only likes, but one that he *loves.* His goal then, is to master the skills of his profession because he knows that, in every profession, there are those professionals who, due to their characteristics, are considered to be the best of the best or cream of the crop. In his mind the killer seals his fate by deciding to be the *best* and most notorious serial killer of his time, while murdering the *most* victims, in his field of expertise. In his quest for superiority and adulation, it is not uncommon for him to compare personal stature to the professionalism of someone like former vice presidential candidate John Edwards who, in his professional circle, is considered to be the best of the best litigating attorney in his field. Ironically, his field of practice is personal injury.

As sinister and macabre as this may sound, this individualistic modality, mentally puts the serial killer a cut above his peers as well as the police. Personality traits, for the killer therefore, distinguish this individual from the rest. Or does it? According to the Crime Classification Manual the serial murderer in this context, is titled Sadistic Murder (134) and Personal Cause Homicide (120). "A sexual sadist is someone who has established an enduring pattern of sexual arousal in response to sadistic imagery. Sexual gratification is obtained from torture involving excessive mental and physical means." (Douglas, Burgess, and Ressler 1997, 136) Jeffrey Dahmer is the epitome of a sexual sadist. Personal cause homicide encompasses "homicide motivated by personal cause ... an act ensuing from interpersonal aggression and results in death to person(s) who may not know each other; the result of an underlying emotional conflict that propels the offender to kill." (Douglas, Burgess and Ressler 1997, 72) John Wayne Gacey and Gary Ridgeway, amongst others, are some of the most notorious of personal homicide murderers. Several interviews with serial killers have been conducted by the FBI criminologists, two of these killers were: Edmund Kemper and Herbert Mullin. Interestingly, they found that: *first,* most "have an above average intelligence," *second*, most "are white males." (Schechter 2003, 22) Additional studies show, *third*, their ages are usually "between 25 and 35 years old ... *fourth,* from high income or low income ... *fifth,* usually married with children and a career." (Serial Killers 2004) Even though he possesses coping skills or defense mechanisms of "denial, splitting, projections, rationalization and projective identification" (Vaknin 2002, 6) in actuality, they are common defense mechanisms of us all; although to what degree, may be the key.

It is at this point in the life of his profession, that the serial killer "feels immune to consequences of his own actions." (Vaknin, 2002, 6) Elated that he himself reads in other articles, that his IQ is in "the 'bright normal' range" (Common Characteristics 2004) the serial killer now gloats as he is convinced that he has chosen the right profession. As he strives to further perfect his craft to his own satisfaction, identifiable characteristics of his killings eventually become: "separate 'serial', occurring with greater or less frequency, often escalating over a period of time, sometimes years, and will continue until the killer is taken into custody, dies, or is himself … killed." (The Mind of a Serial Killer 2004) Also, because they "plan their murders, often travel long distances between their crimes, kill for idiosyncratic reasons, and frequently wait months between killings, serial murderers are difficult to apprehend." (Generalized Characteristics, 2004) In addition to usually one on one murder, the serial killer may now develop a pattern for victim characteristics as he stalks his prey with a "high degree of redundant violence, or 'overkill' where the victim is subjected to a disproportionate level of brutality." (The Mind of a Serial Killer 2004)

Interestingly, it is now, that the serial killer finds himself developing his own: patterns, habits, customs, and rituals, of his craft to reinforce a mode of continuity or discontinuity. Because he believes he accomplishes this with what he perceives as above normal IQ, the serial killer soon learns that his 'precision,' has typecast him into one of two typological categories: *Organized or Disorganized.* (see Table 2.1) Organized serial killers, such as John Gacey and Ted Bundy are those serial killers whose murders "are premeditated, 'as tools,' planning forms part of the offenders fantasies, victims … mostly strangers [and] a particular type … [since pre-planned], the offender will have figured out ways to approach the victim to win their confidence and … gain control over them" (Innes 2003, 74) The disorganized serial killer, such as David Berkowitz and Richard Chase do not "choose their victims logically. He may often error, pick up a victim who is not easily controlled … does not know or have interest in their identity and characteristics, [which is] evident in covering their faces or extensive mutilation of their features." (Innes 2003, 75)

As the serial killer endeavors to refine and fine tune his craft, he inadvertently learns that, professionally, he has been placed into a sub-category of his elite peers. He perceives this as a right of passage, somewhat similar to that of possessing criteria for professional licensure in one's field of expertise. Sub-types for the serial killer include: the visionary, mission-oriented, hedonistic, and power-oriented (see Table 2.2). *Visionaries* such as William Heirens, Herbert Mullin, Harvey Carignan, Joseph Kallinger and David Berkowitz are those killers who, "hear voices, receive godly commands, pick telepathic messages, or believe they are possessed by demons." (Male Serial Killers 2004) David Berkowitz claimed he "was obeying a demon who transmitted his orders through a neighbors pet dog …

Herbert Mullin [claimed he] heard 'telepathic voices' commanding him to kill in order to avert natural disaster." (Schechter and Everitt 1997, 287) The *mission-oriented* killers such as Vaugh Greenwood, Carroll Cole, Peter Sutchiffe, Carlton Gary and Joseph Franklin fall into this category. They are those killers "who see themselves as avenging crusaders, ridding society of 'undesirables,' harlots, homosexuals, 'foreigners' etc." (Schechter and Everitt 1997, 287) Joseph Franklin murdered thirteen inter-racial couples before he concluded his murder sprees. The *hedonist* serial killers such as Jerry Brudos, Wayne Boden, Richard Cottingham, Tim Spence, Harrison Graham, and Danny Rolling all "kill for the thrill of it ... such killers simply enjoy the act of killing. Sexual arousal is common with this type of murder." (Generalized Characteristics 2004) *Power oriented* serial killers such as Dean Corll, Wayne Henley, Robert Hansen, Robert Berdeila all enjoyed killing by "exerting ultimate control over [their] victims ... they are obsessed with capturing and controlling their victims and forcing them to obey their every command." (Generalized Characteristics 2004) At this moment in time the serial killer can look in the mirror, only to say to himself 'all of these categories are a composite' of himself. Moreover, he could also say, 'maybe I will add these components to my professional repertoire or résumé only to consider changing or refining my methods of operation. In order to fine-tune his method of operation the killer's deceptive techniques are streamlined, while he is consistently perceived, as one of 'us' much like the story of Dr. Jekyll and Mr. Hyde, which "has become popular since we all relate to it, [to some degree] the simple thought of having an alter ego you have no control over, appeals to our human nature." (Dr. Jekyll 2004) Serial killer Gary Heidnik was a master of deceptive belonging and manipulation. He was a self proclaimed founder and bishop of his United Church of God, who "would hold church services for his handicapped parishioners while he kept women chained in his basement." (Apsche 1993, 75) As a closing note to this segment, one can only ponder the words of John Wayne Gacey who said "a clown can get away with murder." (Brown 2003, 151) One can only imagine the smile that this comment would bring to the face of his peers. Gratification such as this is paramount to sustain the ego of the serial killer.

Table 2.1     The Holmes Typology of Serial Murder (Part I)

| DISORGANIZED, ASOCIAL OFFENDERS | ORGANIZED, NONSOCIAL OFFENDERS |
|---|---|
| IQ below average, 80-95 range | IQ above average, 105-120 range |
| socially inadequate | socially adequate |
| lives alone, usually does not date | lives with partner or dates frequently |
| absent or unstable father | stable father figure |
| family emotional abuse, inconsistent | family physical abuse, harsh |
| lives and/or works near crime scene | geographically/occupationally mobile |
| minimal interest in news media | follows the news media |
| usually a high school dropout | may be college educated |
| poor hygiene/housekeeping skills | good hygiene/housekeeping skills |
| keeps a secret hiding place in the home | does not usually keep a hiding place |
| nocturnal (nighttime) habits | diurnal (daytime) habits |
| drives a clunky car or pickup truck | drives a flashy car |
| needs to return to crime scene for reliving memories | needs to return to crime scene to see what police have done |
| may contact victim's family to play games | usually contacts police to play games |
| no interest in police work | a police groupie or wanabee |
| experiments with self-help programs | doesn't experiment with self-help |
| kills at one site, considers mission over | kills at one site, disposes at another |
| usually leaves body intact | may dismember body |
| attacks in a "blitz" pattern | attacks using seduction into restraints |
| depersonalizes victim to a thing or it | keeps personal, holds a conversation |
| leaves a chaotic crime scene | leaves a controlled crime scene |
| leaves physical evidence | leaves little physical evidence |
| responds best to counseling interview | responds best to direct interview |

Table 2.2    The Holmes Typology (Part II)

| Characteristic | Visionary | Missionary | Comfort | Lust | Thrill | Power/Control |
|---|---|---|---|---|---|---|
| Controlled crime scene | No | Yes | Yes | Yes | Yes | Yes |
| Overkill | Yes | No | No | Yes | No | No |
| Torture | No | No | No | Yes | Yes | Yes |
| Body moved | No | No | No | Yes | Yes | Yes |
| Specific victim | No | Yes | Yes | Yes | Yes | Yes |
| Weapon at scene | Yes | No | Yes | No | No | No |
| Prior relation to victim | No | No | Yes | No | No | No |
| Victim known | Yes | No | Yes | No | No | No |
| Aberrant sex | No | No | No | Yes | Yes | Yes |
| Weapons of torture | No | No | No | Yes | Yes | Yes |
| Strangulation | No | No | No | Yes | Yes | Yes |
| Penile penetration | ? | Yes | Not usually | Yes | Yes | Yes |
| Object penetration | Yes | No | No | Yes | Yes | Yes |
| Necrophilia | Yes | No | No | Yes | No | Yes |

# The Right and Justification of the Profession of Serial Killer: The Motive

*"What makes life dreary is want of motive."*

—George Eliot (Cook 1993, 337)

Self gratification in any profession is a coveted motive for the professional, however, the concept of motive, comes in *many* forms. In the attorney's case, winning famous cases or large settlements is directly correlated to his motive of increasing wealth and notoriety. Consequently, in every profession the professional must accomplish greater and greater achievements in order to fulfill his obvious, sometimes obscure motives. In this context, the professional serial killer is no different than any other professional. How many victims he kills, how well he perfects his craft of killing, and how deceptive and elusive he is, all lead to his motives of: enjoyment, gratification, and notoriety; his profit then is an increase in *status*. Dr. Stanton Samenow, states that the highest form of gratification, with consequential high profit margins, for the serial killer, is: "to reduce someone to a quivering, pleading speck of humanity and snuff out that individual's life is … [their] ultimate high." (Lintz 2004) Interviews with serial killers have proven Samenow's statement to be correct. Results of these interviews state that "ultimately, by depriving a victim of things she or he holds sacred, such as dignity and self-respect, the offender achieves his most important goal, which is to have complete control over the victim." (Hickey 2002, 156) The research continues to suggest that "to have that control over life and death … [gives the killer] a special thrill;" (Hickey 2002, 156) they in a sense, want to "own the person." (Scott 2003) Serial killer John Christie stated that "I remember as I gazed down at the still form of my first victim, experiencing a strange and peaceful thrill." (Brown 2003, 135)

Previously stated in this segment, there are many motives for the professional to perform and refine his craft. Aside from those sexual sadists who enjoy the thrill of torture and control, there are those serial killers, who's motives to kill are actually for profit. Dr. H.H. Holmes was a profit driven serial killer of the post Civil War. One of many plays of Dr. Holmes was to obtain reimbursement by producing dead bodies; when there was none to be found he would supply them himself. In the 18th century, Burk and Hare supplied British anatomists and medical schools with dead bodies for profit and "quickly progressed to serial murder as a way of maintaining their inventory." (Schechter 2003, 269) In the 20th century, there was Dr. Marcel Petiot who killed and disposed of hundreds of innocent Jews as he took all their possessions while supposedly leading them to freedom from Nazi invaded France. John George Haigh made his living by killing his closest friends. "Then by dissolving their bodies in metal drums filled with acid and pouring the ... muck into sewers ... Haigh himself [stated] 'there are easier ways of making money.'" (Schechter, 2003, 269)

It is at this point the serial killer's profession becomes his passion. He now finds himself emotionally immersed in the excitement and pleasure that killing gives him. Now, as with so many other professionals whose job becomes their life, the serial killer becomes addicted to its mere thought, evolving fantasies, and finally, to the *act* of killing. While thousands of people in this day and age claim that their job is their life only to spend every waking hour thinking and dreaming about how to do it better, so also does the serial killer. In addition, the serial killer, like other professionals, such as: Amelia Earhart who said, "I want to do it because I want to do it," (Cook 1993, 339) becomes addicted to and obsessed with the thrill of '*it all*'; to be further compelled by their fantasies that accompany '*it*'. "So strong is this compulsion, that the serial killer murders to preserve the addiction; ... much of the addiction's allure becomes evident, as does the addicted individual's continued return to it." (Anderson 1994, 4) As the addiction strengthens and his urge to pacify his craving increases, the serial killer is now faced with the intensity of his own being. This is the juncture when the killer, like any one else who is addicted to his profession, drugs, alcohol etc., finds himself out of proverbial control. Interestingly enough, most individuals who are in this bracket know they are out of control or are cognizant of the level of intensity in which they are at, and choose 'to do it' *anyway*. Consequently, their passion for their addiction increases at which point anything or anyone can trigger the killer, into killing again and again. "The triggering factor [criminologist's state] is often a specific type of victim, one who has the kinds of qualities that turn the killer on." (Schechter 2003, 281) Serial killer Ed Gein was triggered by heavy, middle-aged women who usually resembled his mother. Ted Bundy was triggered by young women, with long brunette hair parted in the middle; they were all college co-eds. Jeffrey Dahmer was drawn to young muscular men, while Wayne Williams was enticed by killing poor, young black boys. Robert Hansen was triggered by prostitutes and nude dancers while Larry Jean Bell was triggered by young teenage girls walking or driving alone. H.H. Holmes, M.D. was triggered by any tourist who rented one of his rooms; Albert Fish was triggered by children of the slums. Wesley Allan Dodd was triggered by young boys at the camp where he worked. Indicative of the addiction to murder and consistent with the 'trigger factor' Dodd stated "the thoughts of killing children are exciting to me." (Schechter 2003, 282) Ironically, while Ted Bundy was obsessed with intrigue, as he was assisting the police in finding the Green River Killer, Gary Ridgeway was triggered to kill "young women who could easily be isolated and who were not likely to be tracked down immediately after dropping out of sight ... [the victims were all] prostitutes, runaways, and transients." (Everitt 1993, 238)

Interestingly enough, excellent portrayals of the 'triggering factor' have been depicted in several classic movies. In the 1931 movie *M*, serial killer Franz Becker was portrayed by Peter Lorre. The expression on the face of the killer is indicative of a triggering effect when he lustfully watches a young girl as she walks down the street. The movies *Psycho* and *Texas Chainsaw Massacre* were inspired by Edward Gein who chose innocent unassuming women, usually traveling alone. The efforts of Thomas Harris triggered, if you will, the movies *Silence of the Lambs, Red Dragon, Manhunter* and *Hannibal.* Harris, the 'monster of Florence' was provoked by couples making love in their cars. The movie *Hansel and Gretel* mirrored the life of Marti Enriqueta, who murdered only small children. Gilles de Rais the 'bluebeard' of the 15th century killed only his six wives. Jack the Ripper, the all time favorite amongst the media circles, was triggered by prostitutes. "There were no less than 25 motion pictures, 11 movies, 9 television shows and 1 opera, portraying the atrocities of this serial killer." (Newton 2000, 1st ed. 59)

## The Act in the Art of the Profession: The Mode

> *"Things are in their essence what we choose to make them. A thing is, according to the mode in which one looks at it."*
>
> —Oscar Wilde (Cook 1993, 536)

At this juncture, the continuous practicing and refining of the act is paramount in the serial killer's profession. Just as a professional seeks to learn new techniques of his craft, he subsequently tests and practices them to see if they work better. Professional golfers are notorious for experiencing this phenomenon; as their swing seems, 'satisfying' there is always something else they can try in order to improve it: whether it is buying a new golf club or change in stance, etc. Therefore, the essence of this behavior is the mode or actions that change, in order to attain a certain goal. In this respect, the professional serial killer is no different than the golfer, or any other professional, for that matter. According to the Crime Classification Manual these types of actions are called the mode of operation or the *Modus Operandi.* The *MO* or mode, is obtained from trial and error experiences learned from the practice of murder, for the serial killer. "The modus operandi is very dynamic and malleable. During his criminal career an offender usually modifies the MO as he gains experience." (Douglas, Burgess and Ressler 1997, 260) Further, it is the ending result of the killer's actions and the victims' responses to them that ultimately encourage the killer to modify, upgrade or down-grade his modus operandi. If the victim struggled during her victimization the killer will then bring a rope or duct tape to the next crime scene; if the killer had trouble entering a house, he will learn how to pick locks. If whatever he attempts to change does not work for him, the killer may easily decide to change his MO to include either a "blitz-attack … or resort to greater violence." (Douglas, Burgess and Ressler 1997, 260) Whenever the serial killer attempts to change his MO, the ultimate goal is the drive for perfection in all areas of the act itself. It is with the modus operandi, constantly on the mind of the serial killer, that obsessively keeps him thinking and fantasizing about the next time, and the time after that. The significance about this thought, is that it is not unlike any other professional, such as a golfer, who wishes to improve his game only to, for example purchase a new driver, while, he repeatedly fantasizes and pictures in his mind practicing and playing with it in tournaments. As the professional golfer continues to take lessons, so does the serial killer as he continues to learn, refine, and develop new and unique skill as he plans more murders. Jeffrey Dahmer decided to change his MO from initially beginning with the murdering, dismembering, and disposing the body parts of his first victim only to graduate to drugging, dismembering, cannibalizing, and collecting the bones of his victims as he kept the decomposed body parts in vats. His final, yet most significant development of his MO was to "lobotomize some of his victims by pouring muriatic acid through drilled holes and into their brain tissues." (Hickey 2002, 113) Ted Bundy began his killing spree with the MO of voyeurism, peeping through windows while watching women undress. He graduated from voyeurism to stalking and attacking women with a blunt instrument such as a wooden club or tire iron. As he sodomized and sexually mutilated some, Bundy eventually changed his MO to include: sleeping with, having sex, and biting the bodies of his victims. In some cases Bundy graduated to keeping "the bodies of his victims for days and is believed by some investigators to have shampooed the hair of and applied make up to more than one victim." (Hickey 2002, 165)

Subsequent to fine-tuning his MO, the killer now realizes that he is temporarily pleased and comfortable with his revisions which ultimately evolve into a personal pattern of killing. This pattern then develops into the serial killer's ritual, or ceremonial manner in which he behaviorally operates within the content of the act and process of murder. The ritual therefore is a revised comfort level or: simply his new and improved "particular *way of killing*." (Schechter and Everitt

1997, 258) Jack the Ripper, one of the more notorious early serial killers, concluded his act of killing with what resembled "ritual evisceration, as if in a primitive sacrifice … offering the victims entrails to the gods … [John Wayne Gacey] … turned his … murders into grotesque ceremony by reciting the Twenty-Third Psalm (The Lord Is My Shepard) while … garroting his victims." (Schechter and Everitt 1997, 258) Ed Gein unknowingly fashioned himself to the Aztec priests who clothed themselves with the flayed skin of sacrificial victims. Gein emulated this ritual and "liked to parade around in apparel fashioned from human flesh of dissected female corpses." (Schechter, 2003, 246) Albert De Salvo … "ritualistically left his victims looking like grotesque, gift-wrapped holiday presents." (Schechter and Everitt 1997, 259) Jeffrey Dahmer was in the process of designing a shrine, that already included "cleaned skulls which had been spray painted black and silver," (Hickey 2002, 113) waiting to be encompassed into the details of the design. According to several interviews with serial killers, FBI profiler, John Douglas states that, an addendum to the killer's ritual, is that if the killer cannot find any victims, he will customarily "return to the previous [killing] site … and role in the fantasy of the murder." (Olsaker and Klein 1992)

Consequently, the *Hunt* is another component of the serial killer's modus operandi, one that he may or may not, wish to change. The hunt basically means the manner in which the hunter finds his prey. For the serial killer, the hunt is of the utmost importance, because it adds to the thrill of his profession. Wesley Alan Dodd, who killed three children in "Washington in 1989, wrote in his diary 'now ready for my second day of the hunt; will start at about 10 a.m. and take a lunch so I don't have to return home.'" (Innes 2003, 157) As a result of additional interviews with serial killers, categories have been devised to further clarify their MO's. These categories include: the hunter, poacher, troller and the trapper. The *hunter* is one who begins his hunt starting from his residence; *poacher*, is one who travels or commutes to find his victims; *troller*, is one who inadvertently kills while involved in other activities; *trapper*, is one who finds an acceptable position, occupation or situation in which to stake out his prey. There are also three kinds of attackers: the raptor, stalker, and the ambusher. The *captor* instantly attacks his prey; the *stalker*, watches and waits while advancing closer and closer to his prey, while the *ambusher* attacks his prey after the victim has been lured to a certain location. It is intriguing to notice that as some of the serial killers, such as Ted Bundy began his killing spree, he eventually changed his MO from attacking and abducting his victims to preying on their vulnerability while luring them to his car. Similar to where the professional of any profession learns to find his clients, patients, or customers so does the serial killer who is learning to hunt for victims. David Berkowitz 'the Son of Sam' commented "I love to hunt. Prowling the streets looking for fair game—tasty meat ... I live for the hunt." (Schechter 2003, 283) Jack the Ripper committed his atrocities in the White Chapel slum district in London; David Berkowitz killed his victims in the boroughs of New York; John Wayne Gacey hunted for his victims in the Greyhound Bus Station; Jeffrey Dahmer found his victims in gay bars; and Angel Maturino Resendiz found his victims along the railway line he rode.

Because "they see other people as mere tools for their own," (Lintz 2004) the serial killer perceives them as mere objects or simply tools of their trade. Consequently, the objectification of the victim eases the killer's act of killing. His perspective of the victim is none other than a means to an end. In the mind of the serial killer, the 'end' means *whatever* he utilizes to fulfill his own pleasure; and how he attains these means, either by: strangulation, mutilation, cannibalism, or torture. The ultimate goal is always, his obsessive, compulsion which drives him to replenish his needs.

An additional dimension referencing the art of the serial killer's profession is worth mentioning. The first dimension is one of trophies, the second is taunts. Trophies, in the writer's perspective, symbolize a kind of reimbursement for the serial killer, an article of the victim that he utilizes to reminisce. In actuality they are mementos; symbolizing and representing the conquering of his prey as tokens of the hunt. Interestingly enough, warriors, of all ages have collected souvenirs from their fallen foes. Edward Gein hung human heads on his bedroom wall and when boys from the community asked him what they were he replied they were "shrunken South Sea heads, sent by a cousin who had fought in the Philippines in the Second World War." (Schechter 2003, 328) Other items collected by serial killers include, "snapshots, driver's license, jewelry ... clothing, including body parts," (Newton 2000, 1st ed. 220) in addition to decapitated heads, hands, etc.

In the serial killers continuous effort to raise the bar of his profession, it is not uncommon for some to taunt their pursuers, the media, and those related to the victims. Jack the Ripper was well known for sending the police letters offering, next time, to send body parts. The Zodiac Killer sent a letter to the editor of the San Francisco Chronicle, in it was a "bloody swatch of fabric he had removed from the victims' shirt." (Schechter 2003, 320) Albert Fish wrote a letter to the mother of a twelve year old little girl that he had just killed. In his letter Fish "felt impelled to [outline] the outrages he had perpetrated on the child ... fortunately ... she [the mother] was functionally illiterate." (Schechter 2003, 323)

# Perfecting the Art of the Profession: Victim Choice and Victim Characteristics

*"I preyed upon the weak, the harmless, and the unsuspecting."*

—Carl Panzram (Cook 1993, 57)

As the serial killer continues to perfect and refine his artwork, he consistently finds it compelling to select those individuals of the human race that he can easily hunt down and kill. Therefore, *first:* it is not unusual for the serial killer to hunt within their own ethnic group. The reason for this is because the victims that he chooses are in the killer's "comfort zone" (Brown 2003, 65) that is: an emotional or logistical area in which the killer is very familiar and at ease with, while conducting his hunt for victims. *Second,* most victims who happen to look alike, are actually assumptions of the media, even though it is true that the killer usually has an attraction to a particular type of victim. *Third,* "teenage girls and young women … pretty if they can get 'em … are choice victims because they lack confidence in fighting and experience in fighting back." (Brown 2003, 68) Serial killer Edmund Kemper stated "one side of me says, I'd like to talk to her, date her, the other side of me says, I wonder how her head would look on a stick?" (Brown 2003, 69) *Fourth,* elderly women are prime potential targets for victimization especially for most serial killers who are less experienced and without transportation. *Fifth,* the easily accessed victims and those who would not be missed such as hitchhikers, prostitutes, runaways, and drug addicts, are those in most danger to become fallen victims of serial killers. *Sixth,* women who frequent bars, especially alone, are extremely vulnerable for attack. *Seventh,* women who frequent isolated places are placing themselves at high risk for serial killer victimization; joggers are among those potential victims. *Eighth,* time of day is prime concern for the killer because accessibility and anonymity increases as the victims logistically place themselves at prime times for victimization; usually night time, but that depends on ease of access. *Ninth,* children are prime targets of serial killers because they are helpless, fragile and portable. *Tenth,* there are times when the serial killer is a family member or acquaintance of their potential victim, but the odds are slim that they will be killed because they do not want to be caught. The percentages of serial killers to victimization, for example, "family, acquaintances, and strangers in the United States, 1800-1995" (Hickey 2002, 144) is also intriguingly demonstrated. (see Table 2.3) Additional percentages in rank order of "types of victims selected by male serial killers" (Hickey 2002, 144) are also depicted. (see Table 2.4)

Table 2.3  Percentage of Male Offenders Murdering Family, Acquaintances, and Strangers in the United States, 1800-1995

| | 1800–1995 | 1975–1995 |
|---|---|---|
| Relationship | Percentage of Offenders (*N* = 316) | Percentage of Offenders (*N* = 150) |
| Strangers | 70 | 73 |
| Strangers/acquaintances | 13 | 16 |
| Acquaintances | 8 | 7 |
| Strangers/family | 3 | 1 |
| Family | 3 | 1 |
| Acquaintances/family | 3 | 1 |
| All | 1 | 1 |

Table 2.4  Rank Order of Types of Victims Selected by Male Serial Killers

### A. STRANGERS

| | | |
|---|---|---|
| 1. Young females alone | 4. Young males alone | 7. Patients |
|   Prostitutes |   Hitchhikers |   Elderly |
|   Hitchhikers |   Skid-row derelicts |   Infants |
|   Students |   Laborers |   Others |
|   Women at home selected randomly |   Military | 8. Police |
|   Women seeking employment | 5. Employers/business | 9. Racial targets |
|   Nurses, models, waitresses |   Gas stations |   Blacks |
| 2. Children alone |   Fast-food outlets |   Whites |
|   Boys | 6. Elderly alone | |
|   Girls |   Female | |
| 3. Travelers |   Male | |
|   People in cars | | |
|   Campers | | |

### B. ACQUAINTANCES

Young women
People in community
People in own group/coworkers/employers
Neighbors
Children
Visitors, transients
Schoolmates
Patients
Roommates

### C. FAMILY

Wives
In-laws
Children
Mothers, brothers, grandparents

In conjunction with the crime classification manual, study of victim character-istics prove to be beneficial. Interestingly, statistics show that in terms of ethnic victimization: "89 percent [are] Caucasian and 10 percent [are] black ... 42 per-cent are ... of the opposite sex exclusively ... 16 percent kill only the same-sex victims ... 65 percent are within the same race category." (Newton 2000, 231) In regard to gender characteristics, studies show victim selection represents 40 per-cent of the victims are based on gender "with female victims outnumbering males by a ratio of 10 to 1." (Newton 2000, 232.)

After the process of victim selection is complete the serial killer's perception and thought processes about his victims are further streamlined and refined. The reason for this is for the killer to maintain emotional distance, to further reinforce his ideology and perceptions of his choice of victim category. Serial killer Peter Sutcliffe stated, "the women I killed were filth, bastard prostitutes who were lit-tering the streets." (Brown 2003, 81) Serial killer David Smith stated "people are like maggots: small, blind and worthless." (Brown 2003, 70) Serial killer David Nilsen described his experience with his victims as "a dirty platter after the feast." (Brown 2003, 28) Serial killer Ted Bundy offered this perspective of the victim: "what's one less person on the face of the earth?" (Simon 2000, 32) Serial killer John Wayne Gacey announced that his "victims were worthless little queers and punks." (Vronsky 2004, 201)

# Forensic Psychology: Criminal Profiler and Criminal Profiling

*"Foolish is the Person Who Thinks he is Beyond Reproach"*

—Bonnie Rippo 2006

At this point in the life of his profession, the serial killer is confident that he will never be apprehended. Because of this attitude the killer may easily make a mistake or leave behind some evidence of his identity. It is this evidence that police have historically scrutinized as they focus on the killer. As they test and retest hair, tissue, clothes, and fluid samples the search goes out for anyone matching their deduction, of possible perpetrators that could have committed such crimes. Until the onset of DNA testing that is: matching genetic chromo-somes of a serial killer's fluids, such as semen or saliva to the victim and the crime scene, several investigations have historically come to a standstill. These cases would end up in the cold case files we watch on television today. Consequently, before the inception of DNA testing, many individuals have been incorrectly charged with murders. Surprisingly, even Ted Bundy, who was a notorious serial killer of his time, was wrongly accused of killing a particular young woman in the State of Washington, just because she resembled others that he killed.

Forensic Psychology, casts a different light on the serial killer; this is the psychological study of the criminal mind as a result of "putting together a wide variety of indicative clues in order to construct a picture of the whole personality." (Innes 2003, 199) Forensic Psychologist, Paul Britton theorized that the mind of the serial killer had to be demonstrated through behavior; Britton focused on the works of Freud, Erickson, and Skinner. It was Forensic Psychologist Hand Eysenck who's theory regarding the serial killer's mind, was "based on Jung's basic distinction between extroverts and introverts … [and] regarded criminal personality as being a combination of hereditary and environmental factors." (Innes 2003, 207) Because forensic psychology has been an effective adjunct to the criminal process for purposes of court testimony, it is highly regarded in psychological circles but minimized in criminal justice circles.

The criminal profiler, usually a seasoned FBI detective, is a welcome yet guarded addition to the investigation of a crime scene and the search for the serial killer. It is with the use of deductive reasoning that criminal profilers like John Douglas and Robert Ressler focus first, only on the victim and the crime scene, as they relate to behavioral patterns of the killer. As their focus is to take a broader approach towards apprehension of the killer, it is *not* their job to apprehend him; this is why their position is guarded with the police. However, what is most significant is that criminal profilers have contributed significantly towards the apprehension of serial killers. As John Douglas has stated "in order to understand the artist you must first understand the art." (Kurtis and Towers 2000) In order to explain this concept, Douglas believes that criminal profiling is a powerful addendum in which to search for a serial killer. According to Douglas, profiling is a combination of knowns and unknowns which focuses on the killer's behavior as it relates to the crime scene; a concept similar to that of the Johari Window. Named after Joseph Luft and Harry Ingham, the "Johari Window graphically describes behavior relationships. Its quadrants represent the whole person in relation to others, and its organization, as well as to individual relationships." (The Johari Window 2003) The first quadrant is the *open self*, which the serial killer knows about himself and allows others to know about him; as he portrays himself as a member of society. The second quadrant is the *hidden self*, the serial killer knows about himself but does not allow others to know. The *blind self* is that which the serial killer does not know about himself but others, such as the forensic psychologist or the criminal profiler does know about him, such as behavioral patterns or signature. The *unknown self* is the most precarious in the hunt for the serial killer, which represents the unknown for the killer himself as well as the profiler. In this instance the killer, spontaneously kills and has no pattern; this proves to further complicate the profile patterns of a serial killer. Consequently, it is all of the unknowns about the serial killer that the criminal profiler must answer. John Douglas states that "I use a formula ... how plus why equals who. If we can answer the hows and the whys in a crime, we generally can come up with the solution." (Ramsland 2002, 193) According to Douglas there are five stages in the profiling process: *first,* profiling inputs; *second,* decision process models; *third,* crime assessment; *fourth,* criminal profile; and *fifth,* investigation; the result ending in apprehension. *Profiling inputs* mean the collection of all evidence from the crime scene. *Decision process models* include the initiation of the question what, for example what was the motive? What was the propensity of risk? *Crime assessment* includes reconstruction "of behavior of the serial killer and his victim ... *criminal profile* [formulation] of an initial description of the most likely suspects ... *investigation* as written report given to the investigators, who concentrate on suspects matching the profile." (Profiling Methods 2004)

Even though the serial killer perceives himself to be a true professional, he at times unknowingly leaves a trademark at the crime scene, this is better known as his signature. It is this distinguishable imprint that differentiates the killer amongst other potential suspects; it also becomes an identifiable behavioral pattern of the killer. These patterns are "extensions of paraphilic fantasies. Sometimes post-mortem mutilation becomes the signature of a particular killer ... [some] collect souvenirs, for example, body parts, [while] ... another cannibalized ... organs from his young victims." (Hickey 2002, 125) What the signature of the serial killer accomplishes for himself is: greater fulfillment of the killer's fantasies; yet, it gives more information for the criminal profiler to solve the puzzle of the Johari Window's unknowns.

It is at this point that the serial killer's professional profile, complete with description of: age range, gender, sex, areas of occupation, manner of dress, living arrangement, marital status and sexual orientation; conclude his professional career, with apprehension.

# Professional Choices: David Pelzer—*A Child Called IT*

*"Life is the Sum of All Your Choices"*

—Albert Camus (Cook 1993, 311)

Research studies indicate that those children who are the victims of "family stress, partner violence and caretaker distress raise the risk for child abuse, which in turn gives rise to poor child outcome." (Salinger, Feldman, Ng-Mak) Interestingly, this is the obvious and acceptable reason several serial killers have used to justify and excuse their personal reasoning for murder; it is also the ploy he uses as a deceptive tactic, to extract emotion from the public while incarcerated. What is significant about his proposal is that the serial killer wants us to believe that, due to experiencing such childhood trauma, he has *no choice*, other than to become a monster and eventual serial killer. The question then is: if this is true then why do others who have been just as abused, choose a profession, other than Serial Killer. The writer's answer is because this is a free country, people choose to involve themselves in a particular profession because: they *want to* and because *they like it.* The serial killer is no different, he <u>*loves*</u> his choice.

David Pelzer was another of the several thousand children who lived through the trauma of child abuse. In his book *A Child Called IT*, Pelzer writes about the brutality of his alcoholic mother. He describes the onset of his abuse, as a *small child*, with experiencing bloody noses, a broken collar bone and being "smacked, punched, and kicked until he crumpled to the floor." (Pelzer 1995, 37) Because he was to be held back in the first grade his mother considered him a 'bad boy' and that he shamed the family; his mother crammed a bar of soap down his throat. Pelzer goes on to describe how his mother held his arm over the flames of a gas stove and continually starved him. By the time he was eleven years old, Pelzer describes how his mother threatens to kill him; one night she stabbed him in the stomach. As he recuperated in the garage he realized the stab wound was infected, as he started to ascend the stairs for his mother's help, he stopped, and thought "No! ... I didn't want to rely on mother or give her any more control over me than she already had ... I brainwashed myself to block out pain." (Pelzer 1995, 97) After he finally recuperated, his mother sent him to clean the bathroom with a mixture of ammonia and Clorox and closed the door, finally let out of the room he "coughed up blood for over an hour." (Pelzer 1995, 109) Later on in the fifth grade Mr. Ziegler, Pelzer's home room teacher sent his mother a letter praising David for naming the school paper, her reply to Pelzer was "get one thing straight, you little son of a bitch! There is nothing you can do to impress me! ... you are a nobody! ... an it! ... I hate you and wish you were dead!" (Pelzer 1995, 140)

> *"Bad times have a scientific value. These are the occasions a good learner would not miss."*
>
> —Ralph Waldo Emerson (Cook 1993, 529)

During his entire experience, David Pelzer learned that his mother owned her behavior. While he chose to separate himself emotionally from her, he decided to refuse to internalize the feelings of hatred she had for him. After he was taken away from his mother at the age of twelve, Pelzer relates that there were some people who "boasted that because of my extreme situation I would end up either dead or in prison—the odds against me were insurmountable. [However,] I never saw it that way." (Pelzer 2000, XI) In his book, *Help Yourself,* Pelzer offers his own philosophy of survival as it relates to choices:

- Don't use your environment as a crutch

- Turn your [experience] into a stepping stone

- Don't give yourself away in the vain of appeasing others

- Make and maintain the commitment of being your own person

- Limit your exposure to negative circumstances

- Above all, it's your life and your choice

David Pelzer chose teaching as his profession, and in 1994 was the "*only* United States citizen to be awarded one of the outstanding Young Persons of the World, in Kobe, Japan for his efforts involving child abuse awareness and prevention." (Pelzer 2000, 180)

# Professional Choices: Solutions to the Problem

*"If we are to reach peace in the world, we shall have to begin with the children."*

—Ghandi (Corey and Corey 2002, 301)

The serial killer who has chosen his life journey through the means of murder is fundamentally no different than that of David Pelzer who chose his life journey through the means of teaching. Speaking practically, both are human beings who made different choices of profession; they were those children who suffered the atrocities of child abuse only to share the commonality of their experiences. The significance of this observation is that the fantasies of both: serial killers, and individuals such as Pelzer, are significantly different. This fact no longer separates the men from the boys, as one cannot separate the man from the circumstances of his childhood.

Childhood therefore is the most influential point in time in the life of a human being. Therefore, solutions to prevent or curtail children from evolving into serial killers are a major task, however, one that can be accomplished. Consequently, options and alternatives to these solutions include but are not limited to:

- Psycho-social profiling of children and adolescents

- Tracking physical and behavioral problems

- Continuous analysis of their value systems

- Yearly psychological testing to be given, and implemented into the end of the year achievement tests

- Education of teachers and parents regarding the 'triad' of warning signs (bed-wetting, fire setting, and cruelty to animals)

- Evaluate patterns of non-compliance, oppositional defiance, and retaliation

- Investigate who their heroes are and who they emulate, also who their fantasies are

- There should be a social worker, psychologist, and nurse in every school in the nation

## Professional Choice: Resolution to the Problem

*"Problems are only opportunities in work clothes."*

—Henry Kaiser (Cook 1993, 507)

Resolution to the problem of children evolving into professional serial killers include: resistance of losing sight of the human element and getting back to basics. This means that because the fast pace of society has led to the emotional and physical abandonment of the child (who is the human element) we have lost sight of what is so important—the family. It is the family as well as teachers, who need to get back to basics and focus on the child. If this would be tragically impossible for one or both then the child should have a mentor to guide him through the experiences of life and down the road to healthy professional choices.

# 3

## *The Career of Ted Bundy*

*"Man does not simply exist but always decides what his existence will be, what he will become in the next moment."*

—Victor Frankel (Cook 1993, 310)

The person who the child becomes evolves then, through the essence of patterns which, in the case of a serial killer, develops into a career. This process of evolution is usually initiated or sparked at an early age of the child, between the ages of one through five years. It is at this time one finds the child in a memorable situation, circumstance or observing someone or something that is either short-lived, ongoing, or both in nature. It is also during this time that the child senses either enjoyment or displeasure of the experience. In addition, the actions of someone and the observations of something creates a sense of interest for the child; this usually results in feelings of amusement and intrigue. Whether the child is not actually knowledgeable or cognizant of what he is interpreting as real, the child does have a sense of pleasure while mentally linking the situation or circumstance together with those individuals he continually views in the picture he remembers. A child who listened to or watched Roy Rogers, Superman, or the Lone Ranger may find himself dreaming and fantasizing about conquering evil and capturing outlaws; while at the same time actually bonding, and secretly enjoying the comfort of a father's more animated yet fascinating and intriguing fluctuations of an unpredictable mood and violent temperament. At its best, this is the child's initiation into a fantasy of infatuation, with no differentiation between men who he now calls his heroes; in reality, the child may actually like the pleasure and feeling he has, while observing the power, control, and dominance those heroes display over others. While the child enjoys this sense of amazement and thrill he secretly dreams of being like his heroes, by play-acting he starts to emulate, imitate, and re-create the person(s) he adores in the scenes he likes the best, in which the hero is always the star. The child now produces, directs, and is in the leading role, of his own secret movie, with always the same theme. Thus, in this context, a serial killer is born.

This evolving scenario was one of many links, added to the claim of situations, patterns, and personal choices, that developed the career and profession of "Ted Bundy: The Poster Boy of Serial Killers." (Lohr 2006, 1)

The war was over in 1945, the years following World War II were exciting, jubilant and prosperous. Due to their heroism, those military men who returned home from the war, were given ticker tape parades, while elevated to the position of American heroes. According to some, the father of Ted Bundy was one such hero of the "armed forces … [was Eleanor Cowell] had only dated a few times." (Ted Bundy: Free Essays 2006) His name was "Lloyd Marshall," (Lohr 2006, 3) a "graduate of Pennsylvania State University, and Air Force Veteran, a salesman born in 1916." (Rule 2001, 27) Interestingly, there are other accounts of Jack Worthington a "rakish veteran of the war," (Michaud and Aynesworth 1999, 56) who captured the attention of Eleanor, a prim and proper maiden of a Philadelphia family, by inference of being "an old-money pedigree." (Michaud and Aynesworth 1999, 56) Accounts collaborating this statement, further conclude that "Bundy himself, once told an interviewer that it was his grandfather, a retired market gardener," (Wilson 2004, 531) was his father. Defense psychiatrist accounts speculate that "Bundy's grandfather, Sam may actually have fathered Ted out of an incestuous relationship with Eleanor." (Predator: Beginnings 2006) When Ted's cousin John questioned their grandfather, Sam, about Ted's paternity he became "volcanic … enraged and apparently acted like a madman; he was wild; he was furious." (Michaud and Aynesworth 1999, 330)

Whatever the case may be, Ted Bundy was born out of wedlock or illegitimate on November 24, 1946. This was an era when the word *illegitimate* was an anathema to women, like Eleanor, who found themselves pregnant. It was also an era that women found it inconceivable to keep or take responsibility of their illegitimate newborn either out of shame or social reprisal. It was for these reasons that a petite, 22 year old, with long shoulder length brown hair, Eleanor Louise Cowell, found herself at the "Elizabeth Lund Home for Unwed Mothers in Burlington, Vermont, [who then] gave birth to her love child." (Michaud and Aynesworth 1999, 56)

> *"The three most beautiful sights [are]: a potato garden in bloom, a ship In sail, and a woman after birth of a child."*
>
> —(DeFord 1997, 54)

For Eleanor Louise Cowell this Irish proclamation could not have been further from the truth. There are various accounts that Eleanor's newborn baby remained at the Lund Home for "three months;" (Vronsky 2004, 103) in lieu of the pressing decision to leave or bring the baby back home to Philadelphia to live with his mother and grandparents, Sam and Eleanor Cowell. The baby's name was Theodore Robert Cowell; the name Theodore was chosen because according to Eleanor "it means gift of God." (Wilson 2004, 531)

The decision to return home to Philadelphia with infant Theodore was the onset of a situation that later proved to be an irreversible series of choices, when a "hopeless" (Rule 2001, 8) and "tragic charade" (A&E Biography) began. The charade involved the additional decision to create the façade that Theodore's biological mother Eleanor, would eternally be known: to him, his extended family and society, as his sister. Subsequent to this, his grandparents would consequently be, eternally known to him, extended family and society, as his biological parents. This decision was made largely due to the fact that the Cowells themselves were deeply religious Methodists and due to Sam Cowell's position as a Deacon in the Methodist Church, they were "deeply ashamed by Louise's pregnancy," (Vronsky 2004, 103) with an urgent need to cover up parental responsibility after the infants birth. Interestingly, the theme of moral righteousness in the Cowell household seemed to deviate from its path when several accounts depict Sam as a wife beater, animal abuser, and hard core pornography collector. According to Dr. Dorothy Lewis, a defense psychiatrist who interviewed several members of Ted's family, including his biological mother, reported that everyone described Sam Cowell as "an extremely frightening individual ... who once shoved his daughter down the staircase for awakening too late in the morning." (Michaud and Aynesworth 1999, 330) Sam commonly "kicked her dog, and was known to sadistically spin the cats by their tails." (Michaud and Aynesworth 1999, 330) Additional familial accounts depict Sam "as a racist and wife beater;" (Newton 2006, 30) his wife who "had been hospitalized on more than one occasion for psychotic depression ... with a long history of agoraphobia." (Michaud and Aynesworth 1999, 331) Another interview divulged that Sam's brothers wanted to kill him.

This was the same Sam Cowell, "a mythic figure" (Michaud and Aynesworth 2000, 18) Theodore "adored ... identified with ... respected ... and clung to in times of trouble." (Rule 2001, 8) It was also in this same household where Theodore and "his cousin Bruce knew of [Sam's] pornography and were privy to it," (Michaud and Aynesworth 1999, 330) in his greenhouse. At this time it is unclear regarding the degree of violent sexual imagery that was poured over by these two children. However, indications of what impressed Theodore surfaced at the age of three when, in the early hours of the morning he lifted the blankets to his fifteen year old aunt's bed while she slept. He then slid three butcher knives into her bed and laid them next to her; she awakened and became frightened. She reported that "he just stood there and grinned." (Newton 206, 30) Interestingly enough, she took the knives downstairs and told her mother, she recalls that "I was the only one who thought it was strange; nobody did anything." (Vronsky 2004, 107)

> *"Children adopt values and develop a moral sense of right and wrong by imitating what they see in the world around them."*
>
> —(Schaefer and DiGeronimo 2000, 47)

At this moment in time, little Theodore had a strong sense that he and his behavior were unconditionally accepted and loved by his parents, especially his father, Sam. It has been speculated, that it was in this era that the foundation for the toddler's personality and character was awakened. Intriguingly the sensation that Theodore so gleefully enjoyed could have been his initiation and right of passage into darkness.

Ted at four

By the time he was four years old "to quote Ted's Great Aunt Ginny, 'we felt Louise had to be rescued.'" (Michaud and Aynesworth 1999, 330) In a time of urgency Eleanor had Theodore's last name changed to Nelson, and her first name changed to Louise. Subsequently, both child and 'sister' were moved, lock, stock and barrel to Tacoma, Washington, where his great uncle Jack Cowell lived.

Both lived with Cowell relatives, until Louise got on her feet; it was at this time when Theodore "reportedly referred to her, as his sister and his mother," (Preditor: Beginnings 2006, 3) but only to friends.

Even though Theodore was traumatized and grieved about moving away from his 'parents,' especially his beloved dad Sam, he found refuge and solace in his great uncle Jack Cowell who was a professor of music at Tacoma College of Puget Sound. Jack was a refined gentleman who's distinguished cultivated nature, exuded a sense of great accomplishment and an aura of extreme wealth. This reality "drew Teddy to him ... [it was] early on when he decided to pattern himself on Jack." (Michaud and Aynesworth 1999, 57) It was not that Theodore dreamed of living with Great Uncle Jack or being adopted by Roy Rogers, not because of their notoriety but because both were "a symbol for Ted of wealth." (Vronsky 2004, 107)

Once Theodore made the decision and choice to combine the personalities of Sam and Jack Cowell into his own, the birth of his own private charade and personal façade were born. Naturally, fueled by being in a state of constant confusion of being taken away from his parents by his sister, Theodore continually sensed "that he was living a lie." (A&E Biography) Feelings of frustration for Theodore surfaced when on May 19, 1951, sister Louise married Navy veteran Johnny Culpepper Bundy, a quiet southern gentleman "from the Ozarks," (Kendall 1981, 24) and cook at the V.A. Hospital. It was sometime, possibly during the reception when now, five year old Ted, "stuck his hand into the wedding cake." (Kendall 1981, 138) Subsequent aggravation fueled his ire when Johnny Bundy adopted Teddy; with another name change he would now and forever be known as Theodore "Ted" Bundy. Ted adamantly rejected this connection to Johnny Bundy, only to consider himself a Cowell, and only a Cowell. Even though the three lived in the same house, the only person he desperately held on to was the exclusive intense bond he had with his 'sister' Louise. He later on revealed that his "early habit of isolation no doubt contributed to his later inability to integrate himself socially." (Michaud and Aynesworth 2000, 22) Even so, the quiet and shy Ted was known to be a good student in elementary school. However, "despite the intelligence and superior grades, his recurrent temper tantrums were violent enough to worry teachers." (Schechter 2003, 161).

Ted in grammar school

The surfacing of Ted's integrated façade became evident at this time due to reports that even though he physically "always felt too small," (Michaud and Aynesworth 2000, 22) he must have felt he was beyond reproach as his teachers described him as "being beyond discipline ... when things went wrong, he would blame an authority figure or the system." (Egger 2003, 143)

Now in Jr. High School, Ted was perceived as a shy, loner, known to stutter who inadvertently portrayed himself as intelligent and more mature from the rest of his schoolmates. In actuality it was his hidden, at times abrupt, sense of superiority and disdain for those he felt inferior to, or otherwise jealous of, that crystallized in these years. In this stage of his life Ted made it clear that he was living in a "house that he hated because his room was in the basement, had never been finished, and it embarrassed him to bring friends over." (Kendall 1981, 24) He was additionally "ashamed of his family's lower class status [and] was embarrassed to be seen in the family's working class Rambler automobile." (Vronsky 2004, 103) He not only despised and felt extreme humiliation, he also "felt acute anxiety ... because of the paltry livelihood earned by his stepfather." (Buss 2005, 222) He now found himself in the very position and situation that secretly appalled him, while obsessed with avoiding and covering up.

Interestingly, Ted was involved in the Boy Scouts, ran his own lawn mowing business, and on the track team. Outwardly he seemed like an all American boy, even though he was secretly teased by his cousin that he was not a Cowell, "bullied on a regular basis," (Ted Bundy: Timeline 2006) and, "was often teased and made the butt of pranks by [these] bullies in his Junior High School." (Ted Bundy: Notorious 2006) In his mid-teens Ted was searching for grocery stores and drug stores to find soft-core pornography. Once again, in secrecy, he would pour over the same images as he once did in Sam's greenhouse. By the age of fifteen Ted would explore the "back roads and sideways and by ways of [his] neighborhood ... people would dump ... whatever they were cleaning out." (Interview 2004) According to Ted, he always looked for and found hard core pornography and detective magazines.

Ted at fifteen

By this time, Ted constantly and secretly fantasized about the images he carefully kept hidden. This young, handsome, quiet and dependable Ted, was an expert shoplifter, suspected in two burglaries, and an avid peeping tom. Even though he always did extremely well in school, Ted was sneaking out of the house at night in order to disable women's cars while he masturbated watching them. Because he was never charged, Ted knew he was above the law. Ironically he now planned of becoming a policeman or a lawyer, but being so severely introverted he "learned to mimic normal behavior;" (Schechter 2003, 161) while at the same time able to mask his fear of socializing by "being aloof, arrogant, and snobby." (Michaud and Aynesworth 2000, 24) Tragically, suspicion for the vanishing of sweet eight year old Ann Marie Burr fell on fifteen year old Ted Bundy, although he adamantly denied knowledge or responsibility for her abduction. Interestingly Ann Rule author of her book *The Stranger Beside Me*, once received an e-mail from a woman "hinting that Ted, a ninth grader, had taken her ... a young teenager to see where he 'had hidden a body.'" (Rule 2001, 547)

Ted was one of 740 students in the graduating class of 1965 at Woodrow Wilson High School. Even though outwardly shy and innocent, classmates report that he was "attractive, and well dressed, exceptionally well mannered." (Rule 2001, 11) Acquaintances unquestionably mentioned that no one had ever seen him date; other reports maintain that Ted had one date during his entire high school experience. This is curious since his skiing friends reported that in a class of 740 students, "if not among the most popular, he at least moved near those at the top and he was well liked." (Rule 2001, 11) Interestingly enough, by the time he graduated high school, speculation indicates that the sudden change in popularity may be the result of Ted's expertise at forging ski lift tickets and stealing skiing gear from the local ski stores.

Ted's yearbook picture

At graduation, speculation abounds that secretly, Ted took pride in a self indulgent right, of how: without remorse or guilt, to make friends and influence people; as he calculatingly "created fictions for himself; suave and stylish Ted, wealthy and successful Ted, brilliant and accomplished Ted, famous celebrity Ted." (Bundy's Childhood 2006, 1) Upon graduation, Ted was awarded a scholarship to the University of Puget Sound.

This was a major turning point in the life of Ted Bundy. The stage was set for him to now fine tune his own personal charade while he continually worked out the façade of his personality that portrayed him as a handsome, debonair, intelligent gentle-man who, with "those beautiful blue eyes," (Kendall 1981, 44) was "marked for success." (Kendall 1981, 25) The only problem underneath this "mask of sanity" (Vronsky 2004,128) was that he continued to display an aura of sophistication and intellectual self-assurance, without the ability to resolve the "flaw" (Michaud and Aynesworth 1999, 332) that so intensely drove him to nourish his hidden self. This internal tug of war was fueled by his sense of inferiority to his friends and acquaintances who represented wealth, position, and stature within the community. It is possible that all he knew, was that he needed to do whatever it took to fill this emotional gap or void. Consequently, what it seems he never accepted, was how to resolve this compulsion without manipulating, using, or abusing others. Subsequent to this position, is that the "flaw" (Michaud and Aynesworth 1999, 332) Ted spoke of, may have in reality, been his obsession with fueling his own sense of pleasure, what Freud called the 'Id.' While he later blamed his killer instinct on "the Entity" (Michaud and Aynesworth 2000, 81) there is some speculation that maybe Ted's immature, child-like play acting self, in actuality was mischievously referring to his hidden but *real* and true *ID-ENTITY.*

While he "explained his crimes in the context of young urban professional ambition" (Vronsky 2004, 141) it was none more evident than his own revelation of being "like an actor in a role ... approaching the victim ... playing a role, absorbed in the role." (Michaud and Aynesworth 2000, 129) The combination of these two ideals resulted in his resolve for a career in deception and murder as he mimicked the persona of debonair Cary Grant in such movies like: *Suspicion, To Catch a Thief, North by Northwest* and *Charade.* Consequently, after studying at the University of Puget Sound from 1965 to 1966 Ted transferred to the University of Washington to study, where he met Leslie Holland (Ted Bundy: Serial Killer 2006) alias, Stephanie Brooks. Clearly the attraction that Ted had for this woman not only focused on their commonality of skiing but his infatuation with "a woman who'd been raised in an atmosphere where money and prestige were taken for granted." (Rule 2001, 13) It was also at this same time Ted worked at the elite Seattle Yacht Club, the Olympic Hotel, a Safeway store, a surgical supply house, legal messenger service, and shoe store; all the while rifling through lockers, stealing uniforms, and taking money from intoxicated patrons of the yacht club. His career of stealing was becoming a state of the art hobby while Ted continued to fantasize over the images in the hard core pornography he so avidly read. Due to this encouragement of his beloved Stephanie to study in California, Ted transferred to Stanford University where he studied Chinese. After a lengthy yet intensive relationship, Stephanie now claimed that Ted was to immature and "had a niggling suspicion he used people." (Rule 2001, 15) Consequently, she broke off the relationship which left Ted by all accounts, shocked and emotionally devastated. Upon returning to the University of Washington, Ted became involved in politics, which embellished his Cary Grant understudy mannerisms. He quietly withdrew from the University of Washington to become involved in the political campaigns of Nelson Rockefeller and Art Fletcher; but politics was not in the cards for Ted, both candidates lost. It was early in 1969 when Ted journeyed to Arkansas, Philadelphia, and Vermont. This trip was a pivotal moment in time for Ted as he attempted to "understand his roots." (Rule 2001, 16) While in Philadelphia visiting family, Ted took classes in urban affairs and theater arts, which proved to immensely enhance the character he was so expertly playing. It was not until he finally traveled to Burlington, Vermont when, after checking his birth certificate, did he realize that he was in fact illegitimate; the certificate included both parents names, listing Eleanor Louis Cowell and Lloyd Marshall. The charade was over, he realized that he had been lied to by his *mother.* In 1969 on his return back to the west coast "he killed his first known victim in California." (Owen 2004, 94)

Ted in Washington

In Washington, while Ted secretly perfected his portrayal of Cary Grant, he met Elizabeth Kendall, a mother of little five year old Tina. As she described this charming man with a British accent, dressed in slacks and a turtleneck, Liz believed that he was her "Prince" (Kendall 1981, 12) no doubt in shinning armor. In order to impress her more this "gorgeous guy" (Kendall 1981, 19) told Liz he planned to attend law school while he, all the while, rekindled communication with his first love Stephanie. Cleverly, Ted enriched his career by returning to the University of Washington only now to strive for a degree in Psychology; secretly, Ted was learning behavioral markers as well as signs and symptoms of deviant behavior in order to throw off suspecting, more astute members of the local authorities who investigated acts of theft in the community. Upon rejection from the University of Utah Law School, Ted continued his attendance at the University of Washington, in a work study program as a member of Seattle's Crisis Clinic where he and author Ann Rule had worked together; Ann worked from 10 PM to 2 AM while Ted worked 9AM to 9 PM. As Ted proved to be an astute, compassionate counselor, he was secretly stealing his school text books and skiing gear. Several accounts attest to Ted's character as a "perfect citizen," (Rule 2001, 187) a man who heroically saved a toddler from downing, also "a man who worked to wipe out violence, to bring about order and peace through the 'system.'" (Rule 2001, 187)

Working at Crises Center

By the year 1973, Ted had graduated with a degree in Psychology, extremely involved in political campaigns, and in night law school at the University of Puget Sound; while at the same time, stealing tools and gifts for friends and family, heavily drinking, and engrossed in bondage, a practice he learned from a section of his favorite book, *The Joy of Sex*. Ted's portrayal as a good citizen, family man, potential lawyer and "lover … of mankind" (Rule 2001, 187) savior of children and defender of the community was his perfect alibi when on January 2, 1974 he enticed Stephanie to marry him, then suddenly broke off the relationship as well as all communication with her. On January 4, 1974 Ted's professional career was in full bloom as he obtained payback and reimbursement from those who he felt and "entitlement [to kill] after what women did to him." (A&E Biography) Cleverly and without hesitation, Ted wrote the script of pleading for assistance, as he directed himself portraying his customary sophisticated role in this venue, as an invalid, using several props including: leg and arm casts, crutches, and slings. As if in an Alfred Hitchcock movie, Ted kept well hidden his killing tools: crowbar, handcuffs, and rope. The stage was set for this young popular, handsome man to begin to abduct and murder several, beautiful women. Ironically, all of these women had the same features of Stephanie, a beautiful, petite, long shoulder length brown haired woman. Interestingly, his mother had the same exact features when she gave birth to Ted. Even Liz was not beyond reproach as Ted once lunged at her while attempting to practice techniques he read about and images he was secretly duplicating in the hard core pornography he now fiercely studied. She later reported that she had found a hatchet, women's underwear, plaster of paris, knives, wrench, gas receipts, and crutches in Ted's possession; upon confronting him with these items Ted warned her that "if you ever tell anyone about this, I'll break your fucking neck." (Kendall 1981, 65) By the fall of 1974, Ted, "was an expert at killing" (A&E Biography) and had moved to Utah where the abductions and murders continued. On one occasion in 1975, while staying in character, claiming to be a plain clothes policeman, Ted attempted to abduct Carol DeRonch. She narrowly escaped from his speeding Volkswagen.

Ted in Utah

No one would ever suspect this bright, young, charismatic law student who now was traveling to Colorado and Idaho in order to kill. Ted later claimed that his heavy consumption of alcohol relaxed his inhibitions which in turn allowed him to more skillfully hunt those women he needed to ultimately possess. He kept up his facade while he was in court after his arrest for possession of burglary tools and abduction of Carol DeRonch.

Utah arrest photo

In order to confuse her identification of him in court, Ted "for three days in a row ... wore different clothing, changed his hairstyle, and wore different glasses," (Egger 2003, 134) it did not work. This was the beginning of the end for Ted. After considerable State ordered psychiatric testing, the Utah judge sentenced Ted Bundy to one to fifteen years in prison. But his suave façade would once again be rekindled, when Ted was extradited to Aspen, Colorado to stand trial for murders there. Again, the pseudo-aristocrat, well educated Mr. Bundy appeared in control as he presented himself in court, acting as his own attorney, who the district attorney described as "the most cocky person I have ever faced." (Rule 2001, 243) As arrogant as he was, Ted intensely disliked being in jail, and informed his good friend Ann Rule that he had read the book *Papillion* four times. Interestingly enough, this novel is the story "of an impossible prison escape from Devils Island." (Rule 2001, 245)

Ted in Colorado

In June, 1977 Ted escaped from a window at the courthouse. He was once again in the limelight only to be hailed as a "folk hero who was capturing the imagination of a town ... where Ted Bundy had thumbed his nose at the system." (Rule 2001, 254)

*"So lets salute the might Bundy*
*Here on Friday, gone on Monday*
*All his roads lead out of town*
*It's hard to keep a good man down."*

—(Rule 2001, 273)

Captured only after a few days, Ted won a change of venue to Colorado Springs where after being in jail for a short while, escaped on December 30, 1977 by sawing through a light fixture in the ceiling of his cell. Ted was a "man on the move ... [who] traveled to Chicago, Illinois; Ann Arbor, Michigan; and to Tallahassee, Florida." (Egger 2003, 136)

Ted Bundy aka Chris Hagen

Now, this once handsome, calculating, gentleman was a fugitive from justice; a man who now calls himself Chris Hagen, a man who constantly changes his appearance. It was one in the same Ted Bundy, when on January 15, 1978 bludgeoned several Chi-Omega sorority women in their sleep. A few weeks later on February 8, 1978, Ted Bundy, who now called himself, Kenneth Misner abducted and murdered little twelve year old Kimberly Leach.

Ted Bundy aka Kenneth Misner

Ted Bundy was now on the FBI's Ten Most Wanted List; according to several accounts, "Ted loved the infamy." (A&E Biography) While he no doubt thought of himself as a superstar, he was caught and arrested on Frebruary 12, 1978 for drunk driving. He was subsequently charged with the Chi-Omega murders and assaults, but the judge granted a change of venue to Miami. Again acting as his own attorney, Ted claimed to dislike the presence of the media in the courtroom. However, he constantly "grandstanded for the camera" (A&E Biography) while he flirted with the so-called gallery of groupies, who strikingly resembled those same young Chi-Omega co-eds that he so mercilessly killed and maimed. Once again, here was the great Ted Bundy, in all his glory, the proverbial Dorian Grey, who to some, never seemed to age, possibly handsomer than before, claiming his innocence as always. While the media proclaimed Ted as the "first celebrity killer, a consumate actor and natural for television, whose face and courtroom demeanor," (Michaud and Aynesworth 1999, forward) mesmerized the nation, while the jury watched on. Unfortunately for Ted, he committed an error in judgement as he directed the trooper on the witness stand, to explicitly explain, with graphic detail, what he saw as he pulled back the sheet covering the body of a Chi-Omega co-ed.

Ted on Trial in Florida

On July 24, 1979 Ted was found guilty and given "two death sentences, and three ninety-year sentences, which would run consecutively." (Egger 2003, 140) At the trial for little Kimberly Leach, once again Ted would rise to the occasion of innocence and self-representation. While he cross-examined long time friend Carol Boone, he asked her to marry him, she said 'yes'; under Florida law Ted and Carol Boone were now husband and wife. The jury returned a third guilty verdict for Ted Bundy, who erupted with anger as he heard it.

Ted Erupts After Hearing Guilty Verdict

Judge Edward Cowart, the judge who presided over the trial sentenced Ted for electrocution; after which the judge said:

> *"It's a tragedy for this court to see such a total waste of humanity that I've experienced in this courtroom. You're a bright young man. You'd have made a good lawyer ... but you went another way partner. Take care of yourself."*

—(Rule 2001, 424)

Ted continued to claim his innocence by seeking several appeals, only to be repeatedly rejected. He continued to bargain for more time, by giving several interviews to journalists and detectives (only while speaking in the third person) about the situations and circumstances in which the victims were abducted and murdered, as well as where bodies were deposited. Another ploy to extend his life, included his offer to authorities to assist Washington detectives in the Green River Killer case. Since he claimed to be the most well read authority on the subject of serial murder, Ted gave valuable, intriguing speculation and insight, into the psyche of this serial killer. This inadvertently assisted detectives in resolving their own profile of Ted Bundy. Finally, in order to attempt to avoid the inevitable, Ted tried to keep the secrets of his victims as "bait … to coerce the families [of the victims] to plead with the court to allow Bundy time to properly confess," (Predator: Last Days 2006) it did not work. On January 17, 1989 the last death warrant was issued for Theodore Robert Bundy. In several more interviews, Ted finally confessed to the murder of several victims and "claimed to murder over one hundred." (Egger 2003, 143) In addition, Ted confessed that he "liked to kill, [and] wanted to kill." (Egger 2003, 144) He additionally proclaimed, that he enjoyed killing so much that he took Polaroid pictures of the dead women because, he explained: "when you work hard to do something right … you don't want to forget it." (Bundy's Confessions 2006, 2) He further explained that "his motivation for killing [was] stealing the most valuable possessions of the established classes, their beautiful and talented young women." (Buss 2005, 223) In retrospect those in the mental health community suggest that Ted Bundy was attempting to establish "some sense of who he was." (Haggerty and O'Regan) His long time girlfriend, Liz Kendall suggests that Ted "was driven to kill." (Kendall 1981, 183)

In the end, Ted Bundy offered no remorse to the families of the victims; nor did he show any sense of concern for the victims themselves.

Interestingly the only apology that he offered was to his mother, who he called moments before his death and said: "I am sorry I've given *you* so much grief, but a part of me was hidden all the time." (Haggerty and O'Regan)

None of his family members were at his execution.

Ted Bundy was executed on January 24, 1989.

# 4

# *Summary*

The profession of the serial killer is one that evolves throughout the life span of a killer. Therefore, the theme of this book is to trace the birth of his *professional* career, and track its inevitable destructive demise. Subsequently, the goal of this journey is not only to understand the serial killer, but to learn how to detect him. Our triumph would then be to set up road blocks and detours for the evolution of future children who perceive their childhood as a right of passage into this *profession*; with a propensity and lust for harming others. Pro-active prevention therefore, is the stop sign on this road through life.

In chapter one the background of the problems of the serial murder and mass murder are discussed with a focus on the rationale behind the serial killer's motives for killing. This section additionally encompasses the answer to the question of why this research needs to be done, with the bottom line of pro-active prevention for the future evolution of additional killers. The statement of the problem attests to the magnitude of the problem as well as reinforces the serial killer's characteristis, typology, and patterns of differentiation that distinguish him from other killers. A discernable trait for the serial killer is his perception of being a victim of childhood traumas, he accepts the public's excuse for his behavior, while he deceptively manipulates his prey; his so called hobby is now a profession. The purpose of this study is to understand and detect; only to prevent this scenario to re-occur by pro-active alternative choice. Therefore, this theoretical framework consists of: research studies, surveys, and articles with professional texts, books, and documentaries, all substantiate the premise of, the term *profession*. This framework also collaborates the foundation of the serial killer as a *professional.*

In chapter two we see the magnitude of the problem as it relates to mass murder and compared to serial murder; this is depicted in global and national perspectives. Historical perceptions and labeling depicted these killers as monsters, etc. while the legal/criminal system declared them insane. As several scholastic entities attempted to rationalize the behavior of the murderers, the psychological forum declared that it was: psychopathic, sociopathic and finally of an antisocial etiology. However, the serial killer has his private personal perceptions and perspectives regarding his behavior. As he deceptively accepts the public excuse for his behavior being the product of childhood abuse, he skillfully manipulates his prey into submission and death. Therefore, in actuality we learn that child abuse is only society's crutch for an explanation, and that the true rationale for him is that the serial killer is developing his profession only with a lust for killing, simply because he *likes it* and none other. As he refines the act of killing, it becomes an addiction for him; he becomes obsessed with the fantasies of killing, where he finds his identify. As with some professionals, the serial killer raises the bar of his craft to that of an *art;* now he deceptively calculates and plans for the *hunt,* capture, and killing of his prey. As his ritualistic *mode of operandi* shrouds the serial killer's actions, he declares that his victims are nothing but objects, or trash; *something* that society will never miss and is better without. Chapter three magnifies the evolution of this process, as the career of Ted Bundy is examined.

Detection is becoming more simplified with the advent of forensic psychology and *criminal profiling.* Deductive reasoning, instead of inductive reasoning, is an impressive tool for the criminal profiler as he utilizes the efforts of DNA profiling to link victim to serial killer, instead of killer to victim. Resolution to the murders, additionally involve the development of a profile of the killer, which included: patterns, traits, signature characteristics, age range, occupational areas, and typological characteristics i.e. organized or disorganized. It is at this point the hunt for the hunter culminates into capture and eventual incarceration or death.

Solutions to the evolution of the serial killer and his profession are: *first,* to realize that he evolves by choice; *second,* he develops his craft into a profession because the serial killer enjoys the act of killing; *third,* he enjoys the act so much so that he prides himself as a professional 'actor' only to literally replay his scenes over and over again and *fourth,* the final act, his capture, is his clever ruse, to claim victimization of child abuse or insanity; a last ploy, secretly to placate and manipulate the public, none other than, for the sake of notoriety.

There are new studies out to detect and curtail the evolution of this problem. We as a society can utilize the energies of the school system to test, trace, and track the warning signs of children having problems throughout their childhood, adolscence and even into adulthood.

Resolutions to this problem needs to be a collaborative agreement on the part of the childrens' teachers and parents to change the fast pace of life and get back to basics which includes the family, with a loving focus on the child. If this proves to be an ongoing hardship, a mentor for the child is an alternative, in order to: teach, model, comfort, support, and nurture him, as he then chooses his path on his journey through life, today and tomorrow.

# 5

## *Conclusion*

It is the sincerest desire of this writer to convey to the reader what a wonderful experience it was as I researched and wrote this book.

At the initial onset of this project, the question of: how does someone justify the right to harm another … kept resurfacing in my mind. The answer came by means of the intense research on the subject. In my final analysis, I have learned that we are all, theoretically, on a value system scale of 0-10; ten being the value system of the serial killer. This suggests then in actuality, we all are no different than the serial killer, if one can perceive him as another human being, and not a creature from the black lagoon. Moreoever, I have learned that *we all* possess those open, hidden, blind, and unknown characteristics of the Johari Window; it is just a matter of degree how close anyone, yet everyone, really is to the number 10 on the value system scale. It is a matter of perception and choice.

Finally, survivors from the common thread of child abuse can take two roads: David Pelzer chose to take one road and serial killers, Albert Fish, Edmund Kemper, Ted Bundy and John Wayne Gacey decided to take the detour. Interestingly even though as the severity of their experiences varied, they *all* had the *freedom* to choose a variety of professions. Moreover, there is no documentation of any known serial killer who has changed his profession in mid-stream, to that of another profession; no doubt, because they all enjoy their work tremendously. To give them the benefit of the doubt, maybe they are just uneducated and believe they cannot change.

In answer to that thought, the writer concludes by saying:

> *"Those who lack knowledge become victims of another,*
> *those who find knowledge and choose not to use it,*
> *become victims of themselves"*

—Bonnie Rippo, 2006

# *Appendix*

Table 2.1        The Holmes Typology of Serial Murder (Part I)

Table 2.2        The Holmes Typology (Part II) Visionaries, Missionaries and Hedonists

Table 2.3        Percentage of Male Offenders to Their Victims

Table 2.4        Rank Order of Types of Victims Selected by Male Serial Killers

# *Glossary*

**Serial killer**—a person who commits a series of murders often with no apparent motive and usually following a similar characteristic pattern of behavior.

**Deductive reasoning**—Moving from general to the specific based on: gut feelings, experiences, and hunches.

**Inductive reasoning**—Moving from specific to general based on: laws, rules, or other observations.

**External theories**—social, psychological, theological and legal ideas and perceptions of a person resulting in assumptions and labeling.

**Internal theories**—personal and intrinsic perceptions and belief of a person resulting in choosing serial killing as a profession.

**Mindset**—taken from frame of reference of events that shape and define the belief and value system of an individual which is determined to set and lasting.

**Frame of reference**—overall context within which a particular event takes place hence is interpreted or judged by an individual and used as a framework for reflection or blame.

**Motive**—a state of arousal that impels an organism, serial killer, to act.

**Perceptions**—manner in which person views an individual, situation or event which ultimately influences or changes the manner in which that person thinks or believes.

**Art of the profession or profession as an art**—the serial killer perfecting and refining the techniques and craft of killing.

**He likes it!**—personal pleasure, enjoyment, and total fulfillment the serial killer calculatingly derives from killing.

**Hunt**—beginning of the ritual for the serial killer to find a suitable victim to kill either by tracking, taunting or stalking.

**Profiler**—forensic investigator who is trained in the use of deductive reasoning to formulate a profile of a serial killer from the victim at a crime scene.

**Profiling**—deductive reasoning used by forensic profiler to investigate a crime scene which focuses only on the victim in relation to the serial killer.

**Scale 0-10**—personal scale of deviation from the norm beginning with benign behavior to that of serial killer.

**Mode or Modus Operandi**—method of operation or doing something-manner/style in which an act is accomplished, i.e. killing of the victim.

**Deception of belonging**—personal term—manner in which the serial killer pretends to be part of the norm; a Jeckyll and Mr. Hyde.

# Bibliography

*Albert Fish.* (n.d.) Retrieved May 31, 2004, http://carpenoctem.tv/killers/fish.html. p.1-3.

*Alleged Cannibal says Victim Wanted to be Killed.* (n.d.) Retrieved December 3, 2003, http://www.azcentral.com/offbeat/articles/1203CanibalTrial03-ON.html. p.1-3.

American Psychiatric Association. (2000) Diagnostic and Statistical Manual of Mental Disorders. (4th ed.). Washington, DC.

Anderson, J. (1994). Genesis of a Serial Killer: Fantasy's Integral Role in the Creation of a Monster. Retrieved June 1, 2004, http://angelar.com/~jeremy/genesis.html. p.1-20.

Apsche, J.A. (1993) Probing the Time of a Serial Killer, Morrisville: International Associates, Inc.

*Are They Insane?* (August 29, 2003). Retrieved March 20, 2004. http://crimelibrary.com/serialkillers/notorious/tick/insane8.html?sect.=19.

*Asylums and Care for the Insane.* (n.d.) Retrived July 3, 2004. http://newadvent.org/cathen/08038b.html. p. 1-6.

A&E Biography. (2001) Biography of Ted Bundy [VHS] (Available from A&E Television Networks) 126 Fifth Avenue, N.Y. 10011.

Beattie, Robert. (2005). Nightmare in Wichita. New York, Penguin Group.

Begley, S. (2001, May 21) The Roots of Evil. *Newsweek*, p.30-37.

Brown, P. (2003). Killing for Sport. Beverly Hills: Millenium Press.

Bundy's Childhood (n.d.) Retrieved May 23, 2006, http://english.ilstu.edu/students/smdare/bundy/tedschidhood.html. p. 1.

Bundy's Confession and Motivations (n.d.) Retrieved July 13, 2006, http://www.english.ilstu.edu/students/smdare/bundy/bundy%27s%20confessions%20and. p.1-4.

Buss, D., (2005). The Murderer Next Door: Why the Mind is Designed to Kill. New York: The Penguin Press.

Carmichael, A. and Ratzan, R. (1991). Medicine: A Treasury of Art and Literature. New York: Harkavy Publishing.

*Child Abuse* (August 29, 2003). Retrieved December 20, 2003, http://www.crimelibrary.com/serialkillers/notorious/tick/abuse3.html?sect.-19.

*Childhood Events.* (August 29, 2003). Retrieved December 20, 2003, http://crimelibrary.com/serialkillers/notorious/tick/event%5html?sect.-19.

Comer, R.J. (2002) Abnormal Psychology. (4th ed.). New York: Worth Publishers.

*Common Characteristics of Serial Killers.* (n.d.) Retrieved May 31, 2004, http://carpenoctem.tv/killers/ch.html. p.1-2.

Cook, J. (1993). The Book of Positive Quotations. Conn: Rubicon Press.

Corey, M.S. and Corey, G. (2002) Groups: Process and Practice. (6th ed.). Pacific Grove: Wadsworth Group.

*Cunningham, Carleton,* (1993). The Devil and the Religious Controversies of Sixteenth Century France. Retrieved July 10, 2004, from University of Virginia Department of History website: http://etext.lib.virginia.edu./journals/EH/EH35/cunn/html. p.1-8.

*Dahmer Case.* (August 29, 2003) Retrieved September 16, 2003, http://crimelibrary.com/serialkillers/notorious/tick/case4.html?sect.=19.

DeFord, D. (Ed.) (1977). Quotable Quotes. New York: Readers Digest, p.54.

Douglas, J.E., Burgess, A.G., Burgess, A.W., Ressler, R.k. (Eds.) (1997). Crime Classification Manual. San Francisco: Jossey-Bass.

Durkee, C., (Ed.) (2005). Hearts of Darkenss: All Americn Hero [special issue]. True Crime Stories. People Specials, p. 119-121.

Egger, S. (2003). The Need to Kill, New Jersey: Financial Times Prentice Hall.

Everitt, D. (1993). Human Monsters; An Illustrated Encyclopedia of the World's Most Vicious Murderers. Chicago: Contemporary Publishing Group.

*Family Tree.* (August 29, 2003). Retrieved September 25, 2003, http:// www.crimelibrary.com/serialkillers/notorious.tick/tree2html?sect.=19.

Fontana, David (1994) The Secret Language of Dreams. USA: Duncan Baird Publishers.

*Geberth, V.* (April 4, 1995). Psychopathic Sexual Sadists: The Psychology and Psychodynamics of Serial Killers. Retrieved June 3, 2004, http://www. practicalhomicide.com/articles/psexad.html. p.1-6.

*Generalized Characteristics of Serial Murderers.* (n.d.) Retrieved May 27, 2004, http://criminalprofiling.ch/character.html. p. 1-5.

Grixti, Joseph, "Consuming Cannibals: Psychopathic Killers as Archetypes and Cultural Icons." *Journal of American Culture,* 18.1 (Spring 1995): 87-96.

Haggerty, R. and O'Regan, R. (Producers) (1995). Ted Bundy: The Mind of a Killer [VHS]. (Available from A&E Television Networks), 126 Fifth Ave, New York, NY, 10011.

Hare, R.H. (1999). Without Conscience. New York: Guilford Press.

Hazelwood, R. and Michaud, S., (2001) Dark Dreams. New York, St. Martin Press.

Hickey, E.W. (2002). Serial Murderers and their Victims. Belmont: Wadsworth Group.

*Inductive and Deductive Reasoning* (n.d.) Retrieved February 16, 2004, http:// www.2.sjsu.edu./depts/ith/graphics/induc/ind-ded.html. p.1-2.

Innes, B. (2003). Profile of a Criminal Mind. New York: Adult Trade Publishing.

Interview of Ted Bundy. (July 27, 2004) Retrieved May 20, 2006, http://www.mobmagazine.com/managearticle.asp?e=160&A=7626. p.2-10.

Invictus (n.d.). Retrieved June 17, 2004, http://bartleby.com/103/7.html. p. 1-2.

*Jeffrey Dahmer.* (n.d.) Retrieved May 31, 2004. http://carpenoctem.tv/killers/dahmer.html. p.1-2.

Kellerman, J., (1999). Savage Spawn: Reflections on Violent Children. New York: The Ballantine Publishing Group.

Kendall, E., (1981). The Phanton Prince: My Life with Ted Bundy. Washington: Madrona Publishers.

Keppel, R.D. (1995) The Riverman, New York: Simon & Schuster.

Keppel, R.D. (1997) Signature Killers, New York: Simon & Schuster.

Kluger, J., and Song, S. (2002, August 19). Solutions and Biplor. *Time.* 39-51.

Kurtis, B., and Towers, J. (Producers). (2000). Collector's Choice A&E (Vol.I-IV) [VHS] (Available from A&E Televison Networks), 126 Fifth Avenue, New York, NY 10011.

Lintz, Deborah, *The Mind of a Criminal:* The *Psychology of a Murderer* (transcript) (n.d.) Retrieved May 27, 2004, http://www.wch8.com/newsroom/healthyforlife/1848.shtml. p.1-6.

Lohr, D., (n.d.) Retrieved June 27, 2006, http://crimemagazine.com/ted_bundy.html. p.1-6.

*Male Serial Killers.*(n.d.) Retrieved May 27,2004, http://www.faculty.ncwc.edu/toconnor/428/428/ect10.html. p.1-9.
Marx, T. (Producer), and Gerolmo, C. (Director). (1995). *Citizen X* [VHS] (Available from Time Warner Entertainment), 1100 Avenue of the Americas, New York, NY 10036.

Michaud, S., and Aynesworth, H., (1999). The Only Living Witness. Texas: Authorlink Press.

Michaud, S. and Aynesworth, H., (2000). Ted Bundy Conversations with a Killer. Texas: Authorlink Press.

*Natural Born Killers.* (August 29, 2003) Retrieved November 14, 2003, http://www.crimelibrary.com/serialkillers/notorious/tick/killers9.html?sect.=19.

*Nelson, P.* (n.d.) Dr. Jekyll and Mr. Hyde: A Commentary. Retrieved June 10, 2004, http://www.wsu.edu/~delahoyd/jekyll.hyde.html p.1-2.

Newton, M. (2000). The Encyclopedia of Serial Killers, (lst ed.) New York, Checkmark Books.

Newton, M. (2006). The Encyclopedia of Serial Killers. (2$^{nd}$ ed.) New York, Checkmark Books.

Olshaker, M. and Klein, L. (Producers), (1992). Mind of a Serial Killer [VHS]. (Available from WGBH Educational Foundation) P.O. Box 2284, South Burlington, VT 05407.

Owen, D. (2004). Criminal Minds: The Science and Psychology of Profiling, New York, Barnes and Noble.

Pelzer, D. (1995). A Child Called "It". Omaha Press.

Pelzer, D. (2000). Help Yourself: A Three Step Plan for Turning Adversity Into Triumph. New York: Penquin Group.

Peraino, K., and Thomas, E. (2003, January 27). Father, Where Art Thou. *Newsweek,* 54-56.

Predator: Beginnings (n.d.) Retrieved May 30, 2006, http://tedbundy.150m.com/part1.html. p.1.

Predator: Last Days (n.d.) Retrieved May 30, 2006, http://tedbundy.150m.com/part6.html. p.1-2.

*Profiling Methods.* (n.d.) Retrieved May 27, 2004, from http://www.criminalprofiling.cl/methodoverview.html. p.1-3.

*Psychopaths?* (August 29, 2003). Retrieved October 22, 2003, http://www.crimelibrary.com/serialkillers/notorious/tick/psych6.html?sect=19.

*Psychopathy: An Evolutionary Perspective.* (n.d.) Retrieved June 2, 2004, http://www.criminalprofiling.com/article.php?sid=289. p.1-8.

Publication Manual of the APA, 5th edition, American Psychological Association, 2001.
Ramsland, K. (2002). The Criminal Mind. Cincinnati: F&W Publications, Inc.

Ramsland, K. (2005). The Human Predator: A Historical Chronicle of Serial Murder and Forensic Investigation. New York: The Berkley Publishing Group.

Rule, A., (2001). The Stranger Beside Me. New York, Signet: 20th Edition.

*Rutigliano, A.* (n.d.) Predestined Serial Killers. Retrieved June 3, 2004, http://serendip.brynmar.edu/bb/neuro/neuro03/web1/arutigliamo.html. p.1-4.

Salzinger, Susanne; Feldman, Richard, S.; Ng-Mak, Daisy S.; Mojica, Elena; Stockhammer, Tanya; Rosario, Margaret. "Effects of Partner Violence and Physical Child Abuse on Child Behavior: A Study of Abused and Comparison Children." *Journal of Family Violence,* 17.1 (March 2002) 23-52.

Samenow, S., and Yochelson, S. (1984). Inside the Criminal Mind. New York: Crown Publishing.

Schaefer, C., and DiGeronimo, T. (2000). Ages and Stages: A Parents Guide to Normal Childhood Development. New York: John Wiley and Sons, Inc.

Schechter, H. (2003). The Serial Killer Files. New York: Random House Publishing.

Schechter, H. and Everitt, D. (1997). The A to Z Encyclopedia of Serial Killers. New york: Simon & Schuster.

*Scott, Shirley,* (August 29, 2003). Monsters or Victims? Retrieved, November 14, 2003, http://www.crimelibrary.com/serialkillers/notorious/tick/victimsl.html.

*Serial Killers* (n.d.). Retrieved June 3, 2004, http://www/karisable.com/crserial.html. p.1-8.

Simon, Robert I. "Serial Killers, Evil and Us." *National Forum,* 80.4 (Fall 2000): 4-32.

*Social Evils.* (August 29, 2003). Retrieved October 2, 2003, http:// crimelibrary.com/serialkillers/notorious/tick/evils12/html?sect.=19.

Stout, M., (2005). The Sociopath Next Door. New York: Broadway Books.

Szegedy-Maszak, M. (2003, January 13). The Sound of Unsound Minds. *U.S. News* 45-46.

Ted Bundy: Free Essays (n.d.) Retrieved May 30, 2006, http://www. freeessays.cc/db/44/smu338.shtml. p.1-4.

Ted Bundy: Timeline (n.d.) Retrieved May 30, 2006, http://angelfire.com/fl5/ projectbundy. p.1-2

Ted Bundy: Notorious (n.d.) Retrieved May 30, 2006, http://www. crimelibrary.com/serial_killers/notorious/bundy/2.html. p.2-4.

Ted Bundy: Serial Killer (n.d.) Retrieved July 1, 2006, http//members. tripod.com/~serialkiller/serialkillersexposed/bundy.html. p. 1.

*The Case of Edmund Emil Kemper.* (n.d.) Retrieved May 27, 2004, http:// www.criminalprofiling.ch/kemper.html. p.1-6.

*The Holmes Typology of Serial Murder* (Part I). (n.d.) Retrieved June 3, 2004, http://www/faculty.ncwc.edu/toconner/428/428/ect06.htm. P.1-6.

*The Holmes Typology (Part II) Visionaries, Missionaries, and Hedonists.* (n.d.) Retrieved June 27, 2004, http://www.faculty.ncwc.edu/toconner/428/428/ ect09.htm. p.1-2.

*The Johari Window* (n.d.) Retrieved March 3, 2003, http://www. theselfimprovementsite.com/johariwindow.html. p.1-3.

*The Mind of a Serial Killer.* (n.d.) Retrieved June 3, 2004, http://freeessays.cc/db/ 39/pn1198.shtml. p.1-9.

*Vaknin, S.* (2002 September 11). The Psychology of Serial and Mass Killers, Retrieved May 27, 2004, http://www.suite101.com/article.cfm/6514/95690. p.1-8.

Vronsky, D. (2004). Serial Killers: The Methods and Madness of Monsters. New York: The Berkley Publishing Group.

Wilson, C., (2004). The History of Murder. New York: Carroll and Graf Publishers, Inc.

978-0-595-42384-2
0-595-42384-1

Printed in the United Kingdom
by Lightning Source UK Ltd.
126948UK00001B/106/A